LOW-FAT

VEGETARIAN COOKING

Classic Slim Cuisine

by Sue Kreitzman

THE CROSSING PRESS
FREEDOM, CALIFORNIA

For Natty Bumpo
and
Vicki Kimm

Copyright © 1994 Sue Kreitzman
Published in the U.S.A. by The Crossing Press in 1996.
First published in 1994 by Judy Piatkus (Publishers) Ltd., London.
Cover design by Tara M. Eoff
Photographs by James Murphy
Food prepared by Janet Smith
Styling by Jane McLeish
Printed in the U.S.A.

For information on bulk purchases or group discounts for this and other Crossing Press titles, please contact our Special Sales Manager at 800-777-1048.

Library of Congress Cataloging-in-Publication Data

Kreitzman, Sue.
    Low-fat vegetarian cooking: classic slim cuisine/ Sue Kreitzman.
        p.   cm.
    Includes index.
    ISBN 0-89594-834-6
        1. Vegetarian cookery.   2. Low-fat diet--Receipes.   I. Title.
TX837.K74   1996
641.5'636--dc20
                                                                    96-25945
                                                                    CIP

Contents

Introduction

The joy of vegetarian eating is in its dazzling variety. The beans, the grains, the vegetables, the herbs; if you find culinary possibility exciting, then each time you plan a meal, the excess of it all can drive you into a frenzy. For meat-eaters, it is all too easy to fall into a well-worn rut of fish and chips, sausages and mashed potatoes, or meat and two vegetables (one of them invariably potato). Vegetarians, on the other hand, seem willing to explore the whole world of cuisine.

A vegetarian lifestyle is easier now than it has ever been. Luxurious choice is available in all aspects of the vegetarian diet. Beans, for instance, range from the humble red kidney to the black-eyed, the pinto, the cannellini and several varieties of lentils and split peas, all the way up to the noble black bean. And grains? The choice begins with plain rice and continues through couscous, bulgur, barley, millet, polenta, right up to wild rice. If the supermarket doesn't have what you want (although it often has) the health food store will. And that's not all: let's not forget the vegetables themselves. These days, vegetable departments are botanical bazaars of delight. Comforting roots and potatoes; fascinating fennel and kohlrabi; elegant asparagus and eggplant; succulent sugar snap peas; crisphead, radicchio, rocket; multi-varieties of mushrooms; green, yellow, red and orange peppers—browsing along the shelves is pure delight.

The aim of this book is to help you harness all this glory into a low-fat way of life. Curtailing your dietary fat levels does not mean that you have to curtail your gastronomic pleasure as well. Nor will you need to exist on tiny portions; one of the advantages of a very low-fat lifestyle is that you will be able to eat large amounts, in fact you *should* do so, for the sake of adequate nutrition. You will be able to take advantage of our modern-day food supply and eat a wide and interesting variety of foods.

A Low-Fat
Lifestyle

There are many reasons for switching to a low-fat diet—to lose some excess weight, to get off the dieting "yo-yo," to reduce cholesterol levels, to alleviate other medical problems that specifically require minimal dietary fat levels, or just to enjoy the benefits of a healthier way of eating.

If, as many people do these days, you replace highly saturated fats such as butter with highly monounsaturated or polyunsaturated fats such as olive or sunflower oil, or the artificially resaturated fats in margarines (unsaturated fats are liquid at room temperature and have to be "resaturated" to make a spreadable margarine), then you have not adopted a low-fat lifestyle, you have simply switched from one kind of fat to another. If you need to lose weight or maintain weight loss; if, for medical reasons, you must keep your fat intake to an absolute minimum; if you just want to improve the quality of your diet and enable yourself to eat large portions without ballooning into obesity, then you must cut right down on *all* fats.

There are three components of food that provide calories: protein, carbohydrate and fat (including *oils,* which are simply fat in liquid form). Fat provides more than twice the calories of protein and carbohydrate. The latter two provide 4 calories per gram each, while fat provides 9 calories per gram. In practical terms, this works out at about 120 calories per tablespoon of fat. And not only is fat much higher in calories, it is also metabolized differently: dietary fat goes to body fat stores in an extremely quick and easy fashion. Moreover, diets high in fats and oils (highly saturated *and* highly unsaturated) have been implicated in various diseases (heart and artery disease, gall bladder problems, several kinds of cancer, to name but a few). It makes a lot of sense, therefore, both to help control weight and improve health, to cut right down on fat, but how exactly does one begin?

Making Changes

Skim-Milk Products

Switch from whole-milk dairy products to those made from skim milk. You will be surprised how quickly your palate accustoms itself to the change; in fact, after a while, whole-milk products will seem unpleasantly fatty and cloying. There is a soul-satisfying profusion of useful skim-milk dairy products available in the supermarkets these days. Have you tried non-fat cottage cheese? It's thick, creamy and luscious, and is great mixed with chopped fresh herbs or—for a sweet treat—with a little honey or marmalade and the scrapings from a vanilla pod. Quark (it sounds like the cry of a drunken duck but is actually a beautifully smooth, non-fat curd cheese) is outstandingly useful as well, as is non-fat yogurt, especially if you drain it to make a compelling "cream" cheese (see page 45). Buttermilk, thick as cream, is cultured from skim milk and has a myriad of uses. And skim milk itself, of course, is an excellent standby, especially if you mix it with a bit of skim-milk powder. The powder will add richness, as well as an extra dose of calcium, protein and very important vitamins A and D.

Hard Cheeses

Most hard cheeses are very fatty, but there are no skim milk hard cheeses available yet. Choose medium-fat hard cheeses and use them sparingly. Italian Parmesan is one of the best of the medium-fat cheeses. It has a deep taste, so a little goes a long way. To grate it, put pieces of Parmesan into the blender and reduce to a powder. Store in the fridge or freezer. There is also available a ready-grated Italian Parmesan made with vegetarian rennet; it is worth seeking out from your supermarket or health food store. While you are at it, check out other medium-fat, vegetarian rennet cheeses to see which you like. Use them grated, sparingly, in recipes that call for cheese.

Ricotta Cheese

Cream, sour cream and creamy cheeses (such as Italian mascarpone) hover on the 80 percent fat range. Ricotta cheese, at 15 percent fat (or

8 percent for the lower-fat variety) is an excellent substitute. Strictly speaking, ricotta is not a cheese at all because it is made from whey. It is beautifully creamy and has an exquisite sweetness. Use it by the spoonful in sauces that would normally be made from cream or soured cream. Much of the readily available ricotta is suitable for vegetarians.

Italian-Style Mozzarella Cheese

The Italian-style variety of mozzarella is available in a low-fat version (10 percent fat). If you can't find it, even the whole milk version has relatively modest levels (hovering on the 20 percent fat range), making it very useful (in moderation) for cooking. Mozzarella is a bland, creamy, mild cheese, perfect for melting on pizzas, in lasagna-type dishes, and other Italian delights.

Butter and Margarine

These are virtually pure fat; why not give them up entirely? You certainly don't need them for cooking: this book is filled with techniques that will enable you to cook happily and successfully without them. As for spreading them on bread, good bread is marvellous on its own, so why spoil it with a layer of grease? If you want a spread, use yeast extract, mashed fruit, a little bit of jam, marmalade or honey, or cottage cheese flavored with herbs, spices, honey or marmalade. There is an entire chapter of spreads in this book (see page 34) just crying out for sympathetic slices of bread. As far as "low-fat spreads" are concerned, they may be *lower* in fat than conventional spreads, but they are still *fat*. Although diluted somewhat with water, buttermilk or what-have-you, they are still, as fat, programmed to go directly to your fat stores with heart-breaking accuracy.

Oils

For many people, oils (especially olive oil) are very hard to give up. Just remember, whatever the oil, it contains 120 calories per tablespoon, and—over a day's eating—those tablespoons add up. It is easier than you think to cook (and to cook well) without a lot of oil. Here are a few tried and tested tricks:

No-Fat Sauté Methods

Sauté (pan-fry) in vegetable stock or a mixture of vegetable stock and wine instead of in butter, margarine or oil. Onions and garlic—the basis of many savory recipes—work very well sautéed in this way. If you crave the taste of olive oil, instead of reaching for the oil bottle, go directly to the source: good black olives. Choose black olives packed in brine (or dry-packed) and sliver the flesh off the stones into the pan with the onions, garlic and stock. Two black olives will add 7 calories to a dish (compared to 120 calories from a single tablespoon of olive oil) and the flavor is lovely. Add an extra punch of flavor by putting two chopped sun-dried tomatoes in the stock. Bags of sun-dried tomatoes are now available in many supermarkets, as well as health food stores and speciality food stores.

Pan-sautéed mushrooms need no oil or butter either: sauté them instead in a mixture of sherry, teriyaki or soy sauce, and stock. These three ingredients enhance the natural mushroom flavor in a remarkable way.

Oil and Water Spray

There are times when a few drops of oil ease things along: a baking dish needs to be greased, a frying pan needs oiling, and so on. For such occasions, make yourself an oil and water misting spray. Buy a small plastic spray atomizer bottle (available from the cosmetic or perfume section of many department stores) and fill it seven-eighths full with water and one-eighth with good olive oil. When you need to oil a pan or lightly oil vegetables for grilling, *shake the bottle* first, then spray lightly. This shake-and-spritz method will give you a very light misting of water and oil—the water will evaporate in the cooking, leaving a bare minimum of oil that works beautifully. Aim for the lightest water/oil mist, not an oily stream. The secret is in the proportions—seven-eighths water and one-eighth oil—and in the technique—always shake and *spritz*. You might keep one spray bottle for olive oil and water, and another for canola or sunflower oil and water, for those times when you don't want an olive oil flavor.

Oven-Frying

Throw away your deep-fryer and invest in a good non-stick baking sheet (no big investment really, they are not expensive). With the shake-and-spritz method and the baking sheet, you need never again drown potato pieces in boiling oil. Home-made oven chips are a revelation (see pages 174 and 175 for examples).

The above methods are just as easy as higher-fat conventional cooking methods. Once you get the hang of them, they will become second nature, and low-fat cooking will be no more arduous than any other kind. Very low-fat dishes can be insipid and monotonous; this is one of the reasons so many people have trouble sticking to such a regime. My techniques ensure that this does not happen. If anything, the flavors of foods cooked by these methods are more intense than their conventionally made counterparts. Without the blunting effect of fat, all sorts of magnificent flavors shine through.

Other High-Fat Ingredients

There is an erroneous belief that a vegetarian diet is, by definition, a low-fat one, but this is not true. Not only do oils, butter, whole milk and whole-milk products pile on the fat, but there are other high-fat pitfalls to watch out for, such as:

Avocados

In Mexico, they call avocados "poor man's butter," and spread the unctuous pale green flesh on bread. One avocado contains 320 calories, about 280 of which are fat calories.

Nuts

Just about all types are astronomically high in fat: for instance 1 ounce of almonds (about 24) contains 170 calories, 140 of which are fat calories, and 1 ounce of peanuts (only 3 tablespoons of the wretched things) contains 160 calories, 130 of them fat calories. Chestnuts, bless them, contain less than one gram of fat per 1 ounce. All other nuts derive most of their calories from fat. Chestnuts are the only nuts that are not high in fat.

Salad Dressings

Obviously, these are extremely high in fat, and mayonnaise is virtually pure fat. Dress your salads instead with lemon or lime juice; very low-fat cottage cheese mixed with balsamic vinegar and a dab of Dijon mustard; or just plain balsamic vinegar or sherry wine vinegar.

A Low-Fat Diet, not a Non-Fat Diet

A totally fat-free diet would be very difficult to achieve, and dangerous as well. A small amount (around 3-4 grams a day) of essential fatty acids is necessary to maintain health, as are the so called "fat-soluble" vitamins A, D, and E that are usually found in the fatty substances of our diet. Cutting out *added* fat, however, should not be a worry. Whole grains are a rich source of essential fatty acids and vitamin E; and green, yellow and orange vegetables are a rich source of carotene (from which our bodies manufacture vitamin A). Skim-milk powder is fortified with vitamin D, and our bodies can manufacture vitamin D when there is sunlight. Eat a varied diet rich in vegetables and whole grains, and get some sunlight on your arms and face when possible (no need to sunbathe compulsively—just don't cover up too completely on sunny days, and don't stay exclusively indoors) and the absence of *added* fat shouldn't be a problem.

Very Low-Fat Note

If you have been told by your doctor to reduce your dietary fat levels *drastically* then omit these ingredients from the recipes in this book: oil and water spray (see page 5); any medium-fat cheeses (see pages 3-4); tofu; olives. But do make sure you eat a generous amount and wide variety of grains, vegetables, beans, pulses, skim-milk dairy products, and so on.

The Cupboard

With a well-stocked freezer, cupboard and vegetable rack, a good meal is always only minutes away. A rack full of garlic, onions and potatoes, a shelf devoted to grains and pasta, a collection of ground spices and dried herbs are just the beginning. Explore the grocery shelves for the best of the convenience foods and stock up.

Canned and Frozen Foods

Canned beans and other pulses, peeled red peppers, corn kernels and tomatoes are staples that make the life of a vegetarian cook much easier. The freezer yields valuable ingredients as well: frozen corn, peas, spinach, and filo pastry are excellent products.

Stock

Convenient and inexpensive are vegetable bouillon powders and cubes. For the stock-sauté method (see page 5), pour water into the frying pan, sprinkle on a little bit of bouillon powder, and you're ready to go. A member of the audience at one of my demonstrations called this the "fish food" method, because it looks just like you are sprinkling fish food into a fish tank!

Wine

Dry red wine, dry white vermouth and sherry are important components of a low-fat cookery regime. Onions and garlic sautéed in stock and wine make a rich-tasting base on which to build any number of recipes. Mushrooms sautéed in the "trinity" of low-fat mushroom cookery—stock, sherry and teriyaki sauce—surpass butter-swamped mushrooms. Brisk simmering eliminates the alcohol so you are left with the flavor, but not the alcohol calories. An opened bottle of vermouth or sherry will keep for weeks in a cool corner of your kitchen, so you will not waste the bottle (or feel that you have to drink up the remainder!) after you've used a little in a recipe. An opened bottle of red wine, however, is perishable. A little vacuum pump, designed to pump the air out of the opened bottle, is a handy gadget to own and will allow you to use what you need and save the remainder.

Bottled Condiments

More and more bottled condiments appear on grocery shelves every day. Look for hoisin sauce (a sort of Chinese barbecue sauce), tabasco (hot pepper sauce), teriyaki sauce (a slightly sweetened soy sauce), spicy ketchup, capers and Dijon mustard. A dash or spoonful here and there livens up all sorts of dishes.

Seasonings

Along with the usual salt, pepper and dried herbs and spices, find a good brand of paprika (Hungarian sweet pepper powder) and garam masala (a relatively gentle mix of fragrant curry spices) and keep them on hand. Sun-dried tomatoes add deep but unobtrusive flavor to low-fat dishes: buy the kind that come dry-packed in cellophane pouches as opposed to those that come drowned in oil. Chop up one or two with scissors and use as a seasoning along with slivered black olives. Nicoise black olives and Greek black olives bottled in brine are just right.

Before You Begin

Following a Recipe

Read each recipe through so you know what you need and what you are doing. Gather all the ingredients and arrange them on your work surface. If you are preparing a curry or chili that calls for a spice mixture, measure out all the spices into a small bowl. Scrub, peel, and chop all the vegetables, as necessary. Prepare everything so that it is ready to go. The more organized you are, the faster you will be able to cook, and the more you will enjoy it. It is a shame to miss out on the fun of cooking (and eating) because preparations just seem too daunting.

Vegan Recipes

Recipes with a **V** symbol are suitable for vegans. Where a simple variation to a recipe will make it suitable for vegans, I have indicated this at the end of the recipe.

Freezing

Recipes suitable for freezing are marked with a **Z** symbol.

A Note on Serving Sizes

The number of people a recipe will serve depends on the way it will be used (many are suitable for serving in several ways: as a starter, a main dish, a side dish and as part of a complement of dishes) and on the appetites of those who will eat it. Whenever possible, I have given the yield in volume rather than numbers of servings, so that you can visualize the amount the recipe makes, and then use it as you wish.

In many cases, it pays to make more than you need, then to freeze or refrigerate the remainder for another day. Leftovers are so versatile. They can be reheated and eaten as they are, or they can be turned into a soup or a sauce, a frittata (flat omelette) filling, or a filling for filo. There is something positively stimulating about a cache of yesterday's food, just waiting to be transformed into something new and exciting. Of course, in some food-enthusiastic households, there never are any leftovers. If this applies to you, put anything you want to save into an opaque-lidded container, label it "tripe in prune sauce," and tuck it away at the back of the fridge!

Non-Reactive Cookware

Cast-iron, tin and aluminum cookware will react with acid ingredients such as tomatoes, wine and spinach to produce off flavors and discolorations. To avoid these problems, use *nonreactive* cookware, such as enameled cast iron, stainless steel or flame-proof glass, or cookware with a non-stick coating.

Soups

The soups in this chapter overflow with comfort and big, round flavor. A large bowlful (or two) with a crusty loaf of whole-grain bread, makes a gutsy meal that needs no other embellishment. The non-fat techniques ensure full flavor despite the lack of butter, oil or cream: "cream" soups are made creamy with rich purées of vegetables; soups based on sautéed vegetables are built on stock-sautéed vegetables that have been infused with herbs and spices, sun-dried tomatoes and (occasionally) a few olives. Robust fresh flavors shine through with no muffling fat to get in the way.

SERVING NOTE

In very general terms, one cup of soup is enough for a starter for one person, and 2 cups are enough for a main course. Feel free to adjust this to your family's needs.

Lentil Soup

V · **Z**

Makes 5 cups

When lentils are soaked ahead of time, their cooking time is shortened, and they need less liquid. However, I always find it easier just to throw the unsoaked lentils in, give them as much liquid as they need, and allow them to simmer quietly until ready. Don't add salt early in the cooking, and use bottled water if your water is very hard, or the lentils may never become tender.

7 cups salt-free stock or water
1/2 cup dry red wine
1 large mild onion, chopped
2 garlic cloves, crushed
3 dry-packed sun-dried tomatoes, chopped (use scissors)

1 cup brown or green lentils, rinsed and picked over
1 14-oz can of chopped tomatoes
vegetable bouillon powder (optional)
salt and freshly ground pepper

1 Combine 1 cup of the stock or water, the wine, onion, garlic and sun-dried tomatoes in a heavy-bottomed saucepan. Cover, bring to a boil, and boil for 5-7 minutes. Uncover, reduce the heat, and simmer until the onions are tender and the liquid almost gone.

2 Stir in the lentils, remaining stock or water, and tomatoes. Simmer, partially covered, for 45-60 minutes or until the lentils are very tender. If you have used water, you can stir in some vegetable bouillon powder when the lentils are tender. In either case, season with salt and pepper.

3 Ladle a quarter to a third of the soup into a blender, and purée in small batches. Stir the purée back into the soup and reheat gently before serving.

*Note: For explanation of **V** **Z**, see page 10.

Black Bean Soup

· · · · · · · · · · · · · **Z** · · · · · · · · · · · ·

Makes 7 cups

Black beans (sometimes referred to as turtle beans) are purply-black kidney beans, and a staple in Spanish, Cuban and Mexican cookery. The soaked and cooked beans make a suave and subtle purée, used to advantage in many classic soups. This recipe combines traditions of Spain and Mexico.

5 cups soaked and
   cooked black beans
   (see page 111)
1 quart vegetable stock
juice and slivered peel of 1 small
   orange
1/2 cup dry sherry
salt and freshly ground black
   pepper

TO SERVE
cooked rice (optional)
cottage cheese
1 orange, peeled and thinly sliced
fresh cilantro leaves

1 Combine the beans, stock and orange peel in a saucepan. Bring to the boil, then reduce the heat and simmer for 30 minutes. Cool slightly.

2 Purée the soup in a blender in small batches, then push the purée through a sieve into a clean saucepan.

3 Pour in the sherry and orange juice, and simmer for 10 minutes. Taste and adjust the seasoning.

4 If you are using the rice, put a spoonful in the bottom of each warmed soup bowl, and fill with soup. Put a spoonful of cottage cheese on the surface, and lay an orange slice on each side. Sprinkle with cilantro leaves.

V Omit the cottage cheese.

Chestnut Soup

· ·

Makes 5 cups

Red wine, bay leaf and chestnuts have a natural affinity for each other and come together very well in this festive soup. It would make the perfect beginning to a Christmas dinner.

6 shallots, chopped
3 large carrots, chopped
I large celery stalk, chopped
6 cups stock
3/4 cup dry red wine
3 12-oz cans of unsweetened
    chestnuts, drained

I bay leaf
1/4 teaspoon freshly grated nutmeg
salt and freshly ground pepper
2 tablespoons skim-milk powder
I cup skim milk

I Put the shallots, carrots and celery in a large saucepan. Add 1/2 cup of the stock and 1/4 cup of the wine, cover and bring to the boil. Boil until almost all the liquid has cooked away.

2 Add the chestnuts, remaining stock, the bay leaf, nutmeg, and salt and pepper to taste. Simmer, partially covered, for 20-30 minutes, then cool slightly and remove the bay leaf.

3 Purée the soup in small batches in a blender, then return it to the saucepan. Mix the milk and skim-milk powder, and stir into the soup. Bring back to a simmer and simmer for 10 minutes. If serving at once, stir in the remaining wine, and simmer uncovered for 5-10 minutes before pouring into warmed soup bowls.

4 If not serving at once, cool and refrigerate before adding the remaining wine. At serving time, bring to a simmer, stir in the remaining wine and simmer uncovered for 5-10 minutes.

Creamy Parsnip Soup

· · · · · · · · · · **V** · · **Z** · · · · · · · · · · ·

Makes 4 1/2 cups

Curried parsnip soup, laced with lashings of butter and cream, has become a British classic. I find parsnip purée enticingly rich and creamy enough without the fatty butter/cream dimension. Adding a potato gives body, and garam masala gives a subtler spiciness than does curry powder. Like many of the soups in this chapter, creamy parsnip soup is a deeply soothing brew.

I large mild onion, chopped
1/2-inch piece of fresh ginger,
   peeled and crushed
2 garlic cloves, crushed
6 cups stock
I teaspoon garam masala

I lb parsnips, diced
I medium potato, scrubbed and
   coarsely diced
salt and freshly ground pepper

I Put the onion, ginger, garlic and 1 cup stock in a heavy-bottomed saucepan, cover and bring to the boil. Boil for 5-7 minutes, then uncover, reduce the heat slightly and simmer, stirring, until the onions are tender and the liquid almost gone. Add the garam masala and stir so that the onions are well coated with the spices.

2 Stir in the parsnips, potato and remaining stock. Simmer for 10-15 minutes or until the parsnips and potatoes are very tender. Season with salt and pepper, then leave to cool slightly.

3 Purée the soup in batches in a blender until smooth and velvety. Return the soup to the pan and heat gently. Check the seasonings, and serve.

Puréed Vegetable-Bean Soup

· · · · · · · · · · · **Ⓥ** · · **Ⓩ** · · · · · · · · · · ·

Makes 7 cups

The crunch of croutons against the velvety smoothness of the vegetable-bean purée gives a little touch of gastronomic heaven. The garlic in the soup is mellow and mild because it has been simmered in stock; the garlic on the croutons is strong because it is raw. If you mind the taste, you can prepare the croutons without the garlic. The crunch-velvet contrast of crouton-soup will still send frissons of pleasure up and down your spine.

2 garlic cloves, crushed
I medium onion, diced
2-3 black olives in brine, drained
   and flesh slivered off the stones
1/4 teaspoon crushed dried chilies
   (or to taste)
5 cups vegetable stock
4 cups mixed vegetables,
   coarsely chopped: zucchini, small
   white turnips, carrots, potatoes,
   green peas (frozen are fine)

salt and freshly ground pepper
2 tablespoons shredded fresh basil
I tablespoon chopped fresh parsley
I 15-oz can cannellini beans,
   drained and rinsed
Garlic croutons (see next page)

I Put the garlic, onion, olive pieces, chilies and 1 cup stock in a heavy-bottomed saucepan, cover and bring to the boil. Boil for 5 minutes, then reduce the heat slightly, uncover and simmer until the onion is tender and the liquid almost gone.

2 Add all the vegetables (except the cannellini beans), and season with salt and pepper. Cook gently, stirring, for a few minutes, then stir in the remaining stock. Simmer, covered, for 30-35 minutes, then stir in the herbs and beans, and cook for a few minutes more or until all the vegetables are tender. Leave to cool slightly.

3 Purée the soup in small batches in a blender until very smooth. Taste and adjust the seasonings, and serve sprinkled with croutons.

GARLIC CROUTONS

Dry slices of day-old bread in the oven at 350°F, turning occasionally. When they are dry and crisp right through, remove them from the oven, and rub each slice thoroughly with the cut side of a garlic clove. Cut or break the slices into rough 1/4- to 1/2-inch cubes.

Squash Soup in a Squash

· ·

Serves 1

Acorn squash is one of the winter squashes—sturdy, gourd-like vegetables available in supermarkets during the autumn and winter months. When baked, the inner flesh becomes ineffably sweet and tender, but the shell holds its shape. In this recipe, acorn squash becomes a mini-tureen, holding a gentle brew of stock and cheese, making this a most dramatic—and most comforting—soup. This makes one serving; multiply it to make as many as you need.

I acorn squash
2 scallions, trimmed and
   sliced
I garlic clove, crushed
about I cup hot stock

I tablespoon breadcrumbs
salt and freshly ground pepper
pinch of freshly grated nutmeg
I tablespoon grated Parmesan
   (or other medium-fat cheese)

1 Preheat the oven to 400°F.

2 If necessary, cut a very thin slice off the bottom of the squash so that it sits on a level bottom. Be careful—there must be no leaks in the squash, and the bottom must remain thick. Cut a "cap" off the top of the squash and scrape out the seeds and fibers.

3 Put the onions and garlic in a saucepan with a little of the stock, and simmer until the onions are tender and the liquid gone. Add the breadcrumbs, and stir until the onions and crumbs are well combined. Remove from heat, season with salt and pepper, and stir in the nutmeg and cheese.

4 Spoon the crumb-cheese mixture into the squash. Pour in enough of the remaining stock to fill the squash seven-eighths full, and place the "cap" back on the squash.

5 Put the squash in a non-stick baking dish and bake in the oven for 45 minutes to 1 hour or until the soup is simmering and the inside of the squash is becoming tender.

6 Reduce the oven temperature to 300°F, and continue to bake for a further 15-20 minutes or until the inside of the squash is quite tender. Remember, the outside of the squash must not lose its shape.

7 Taste the soup, adjust the seasonings, and serve the squash, set in a soup bowl, at once. To eat, spoon out the soup along with the tender squash flesh.

Green Velvet Soup

· · · · · · · · · · · · **V** · · **Z** · · · · · · · · · · · ·

Makes 6 cups

This is another velvet-textured soup that cries out for the crunch of crou-
tons (see page 17). This may sound very odd, but if you want instant non-
fat croutons, try bite-sized Shredded Wheat; they are brilliant as a soup
garnish. A handful of freshly popped popcorn (see next page) will happily
garnish a bowl of creamy soup as well.

I large mild onion, coarsely chopped
4 celery stalks, coarsely chopped
2 garlic cloves, crushed
1/4 small green or white cabbage,
   cored and coarsely chopped
I small bulb of fennel, coarsely
   chopped
3 small zucchini, coarsely diced
I bunch broccoli, coarsely
   chopped

1/4 lb. string beans, sliced into
   I-inch pieces
I potato, scrubbed and
   coarsely diced
4 cups vegetable stock
salt and freshly ground pepper
6 tablespoons chopped fresh parsley
4 tablespoons shredded fresh basil

I Combine all the ingredients, except the herbs, in a large, heavy-
bottomed saucepan. Cover and bring to the boil, then reduce the heat
and simmer partially covered for 45 minutes, stirring occasionally.
Add the herbs and more salt and pepper, if necessary. Simmer for 5-10
minutes more, then leave to cool slightly.

2 Purée the soup in small batches in a blender until *very* smooth and
velvety, then push through a sieve back into a saucepan. Reheat, taste
and adjust the seasonings before serving.

MICROWAVE POPCORN

Makes 7 cups

Store corn for popping in the freezer and cook it frozen—the popcorn will be exceptionally fluffy. Microwave ovens are not consistent, so you will have to check the time given in this recipe by testing it in your particular machine. If the popcorn stays in too long, it scorches. Do not buy "microwave popcorn" as it contains added fat. Just buy plain, unadorned popcorn.

1 Pour the popping corn into a 9-inch diameter microwave-proof glass bowl. Put in just enough to make a single layer, patting it down so that it covers the bottom of the dish evenly. Cover tightly with plastic wrap.

2 Microwave on high for 3-7 minutes.

3 Pierce the plastic wrap to release the steam (avert your face), then carefully peel off the plastic wrap and tip the popcorn into a bowl.

Creamy and Spicy Potato Soup

· · · · · · · · · · (V) · · (Z) · · · · · · · · · · · ·

Makes 8 cups

This is a magnificent soup to make in a large quantity and then freeze in individual portions, although you and your housemates might easily pol-ish off a whole batch in a day or two. Although an entire head of garlic is used, it gives textural substance and flavor without harsh vulgarity. The color, a glowing apricot, is lovely as well. If you have no grilled peppers on hand for the garnish (see page 131), canned or bottled red peppers can be puréed and seasoned instead.

1 1/2 tablespoons sesame seeds
1 tablespoon fennel seeds
1 teaspoon cumin seeds
1 head of garlic
3 medium onions, halved and
   sliced into thin half moons
5 cups vegetable stock
6 medium potatoes, peeled
   and quartered
salt and freshly ground pepper
1 large red pepper, deseeded
   and coarsely chopped

1 lb frozen or fresh corn kernels
1 14-oz can of chopped
   Italian tomatoes
1 tablespoon fresh lime juice

GARNISH
puréed grilled peppers (see page
   131) seasoned with a dab of
honey (or brown sugar for
   vegans) and a dash of
tabasco sauce

1 Put all the seeds in a heavy-bottomed saucepan, and heat gently for about 1 minute or until lightly toasted and fragrant, stirring constantly.

2 Separate the head of garlic into cloves. Hit each clove lightly with a kitchen mallet or the flat side of a wide-bladed knife to loosen the skin, then remove and discard the skin.

3 Put the onions and garlic into the saucepan with the seeds. Pour in 1 cup stock, cover and bring to the boil, then reduce the heat and sim-mer briskly for 5 minutes. Uncover and continue to cook over mod-erate heat, stirring occasionally, for 5-10 minutes or until the onions are tender and the stock has almost cooked away.

4 Add the potatoes, stir and cook for 2-3 minutes more.

5 Stir in the remaining ingredients except the garnish, and simmer, partially covered, for 30 minutes or until the potatoes are very tender. Skim off the foam occasionally as it cooks. Leave to cool slightly.

6 Purée the mixture in small batches in a blender, then push it through a sieve. To serve, reheat the soup and adjust the seasonings, then pour into warmed soup bowls and garnish with a swirl of puréed grilled peppers seasoned with a little honey or brown sugar and a dash of tabasco sauce.

Simple Vegetable Soup

· · · · · · · · · · · **V** · · **Z** · · · · · · · · · · ·

Makes 5 cups

This recipe demonstrates how good the stock-sauté method (see page 5) can be: the fresh vegetable flavor, unhampered by any fat, just shines through.

2 medium carrots, coarsely diced
I large onion, halved and sliced
  into thin half moons
3 garlic cloves, crushed
5 cups vegetable stock
3 peppers (I red, I yellow,
  I green) peeled, deseeded
  and coarsely diced
3 small zucchini, coarsely diced

5 ripe tomatoes, peeled,
  deseeded and quartered
  (substitute canned tomatoes
  when good tomatoes are
  unavailable)
salt and freshly ground pepper
3 tablespoons chopped fresh parsley
I bunch chives, finely snipped

I Put the carrots, onion, garlic and 1 cup stock in a heavy-bottomed saucepan. Cover, bring to the boil, and boil for 7 minutes. Uncover, reduce the heat slightly and simmer briskly until the onions and carrots are tender and the liquid almost gone. Add the peppers and a splash of stock, and cook, stirring, for a few minutes more.

2 Stir in the zucchini, tomatoes and remaining stock, and simmer for 10-15 minutes or until everything is tender. Season with salt and pepper, and stir in the herbs. Cook for 1-2 minutes more.

PRESSING MATTERS

Be kind to garlic, and don't subject it to a garlic press, which turns it into an acrid mess. Instead, buy a wooden mallet and use it to crush garlic cloves: hit each clove lightly with the mallet to loosen the skin, then remove the skin and crush the clove with the mallet. This down-to-earth wooden implement also works well crushing slices of fresh ginger root. Alternatively, use the bottom of a bottle or the flat side of a wide knife.

Colorful Corn Chowder

· · · · · · · · · · · · **②** · · · · · · · · · · · · ·

Makes 6 cups

This chowder bursts with color, texture and nutrition, and served with a crusty loaf of bread makes a splendid evening meal.

12 scallions, sliced
2-3 dry-packed sun-dried
   tomatoes, chopped (use scissors)
2 carrots, coarsely chopped
1 large red pepper, peeled,
   deseeded and coarsely chopped
1 fresh chili, deseeded and finely
   chopped
1-2 garlic cloves, crushed
1/2 teaspoon ground cumin
1/2 teaspoon ground coriander
4 cups vegetable stock

3 medium potatoes, cut into
   1/2-inch cubes
1 lb frozen corn kernels
salt and freshly ground pepper
1 cup skim milk
2 tablespoons skim-milk powder
3-4 tablespoons chopped fresh
   cilantro
3-4 tablespoons shredded fresh
   mint

1 Put the onions, tomatoes, carrots, red pepper, chili, garlic and spices in a large heavy-bottomed saucepan with 1 cup stock. Cover, bring to the boil and boil for 3-5 minutes. Stir in the potatoes and simmer for 3-4 minutes more, until the liquid has almost gone.

2 Stir in the remaining stock, and simmer, partially covered, for about 5 minutes or until the potatoes are almost tender. Stir in the corn, season with salt and pepper, and simmer until all the vegetables are tender. Remove from the heat.

3 Mix the milk and skim-milk powder and stir into the soup. Ladle out 1 cup of the soup and purée it in small batches in a blender until smooth. Stir the purée back into the saucepan, taste and adjust the seasonings.

4 Simmer for 3-4 minutes, then stir in the herbs before serving.

Mushroom Barley Soup

· · · · · · · · · · · **Ⓥ** · · **Ⓩ** · · · · · · · · · · ·

Makes 6 cups

Mushroom Barley Soup is a beloved and enduring Russian/Jewish classic. The real thing contains a frightening amount of rendered chicken fat: double anathema for low-fat vegetarians. By any standard, substituting the non-fat mushroom sauté method for the chicken fat improves the classic immeasurably. Whole grain barley (available in health food stores) has had less processing than pearl barley (available in supermarkets), and therefore contains more nutrients. It is worth seeking out the whole variety: it will take longer to cook and will be chewier (this is actually a plus— the texture is wonderful). If you choose to use the easier-to-find pearl barley, cut about 15 minutes off the cooling time.

I oz dried porcini mushrooms	8 scallions, sliced
I 1/2 cups hot water	1/2 cup dry sherry
I 1/2 lb fresh mushrooms	several dashes teriyaki or
(preferably brown cap),	soy sauce
cut into quarters or eighths,	4 cups vegetable stock
depending on size	1/2 cup barley, rinsed
2 garlic cloves, crushed	salt and freshly ground pepper

I Rinse the dried mushrooms well under cold running water. Put them in a bowl with the hot water and leave to soak for 20-30 minutes.

2 Put the fresh mushrooms, garlic, scallions, sherry and teriyaki or soy sauce in a heavy-bottomed saucepan. Cook, stirring occasion-ally, until the mushrooms begin to exude a great deal of liquid and to turn dark.

3 Strain the soaking water from the dried mushrooms through a sieve lined with a double layer of muslin or coffee filter papers, and reserve mushrooms and soaking water. Rinse the soaked mushrooms under cold running water, and trim off and discard any tough stems. Cut the mushrooms into coarse pieces. Add them to the soup along with their strained soaking water. Add the stock and barley, season with salt and pepper, and simmer, partially covered, for 1 hour or until the barley is tender. Taste and adjust the seasoning.

DRIED MUSHROOMS

Dried *Boletus edulis* mushrooms *(porcini* in Italian, *cèpes* in French) are available in speciality food shops and some supermarkets. You need no more than 1 ounce: when reconstituted they plump up to about five times their dried weight, and the flavor will be up to twenty times as intense as 1 ounce of the same mushrooms in their fresh state. They must be rinsed well before soaking, and after soaking their powerfully flavored soaking water should be strained to eliminate the copious sand that lurks in the mushrooms' nooks and crannies.

Red Pepper Soup

· · · · · · · · · · · **V** · · **Z** · · · · · · · · · · · · ·

Makes 6 cups

I can't keep my hands off red peppers—the color, the flavor, the luscious texture of the peppers when they have been divested of their skins, sautéed in stock and puréed.... For this soup, I've used both smoky grilled peppers and raw peppers that have been peeled with a swivel-bladed peeler. They combine beautifully with paprika (a close relative) to make a glowing, restorative soup. Bottled or canned red peppers could be used instead of the grilled peppers.

8 large red peppers
1 large mild onion, chopped
1 garlic clove, crushed
1 tablespoon paprika
5 cups vegetable stock

1 medium potato,
    peeled and coarsely diced
salt and freshly ground pepper

1 Grill and peel three of the peppers (see page 131), then deseed and coarsely dice them. Peel the remaining five peppers with a swivel-bladed peeler (see next page), then deseed and coarsely dice them.

2 Put the onion, garlic and paprika in a heavy-bottomed saucepan with 1 cup of the stock. Cover, bring to the boil, and boil for 4-5 minutes, then uncover, reduce the heat and simmer until the onions are tender and gently "frying" in their own juices.

3 Stir in the chopped raw peppers with a further cup of the stock. Simmer for a few minutes, stirring occasionally, until the peppers begin to soften, then stir in the potato and cook for 2-3 minutes more.

4 Stir in the remaining stock and the grilled peppers, and season with salt and pepper. Simmer, partially covered, for about 30 minutes or until the vegetables are very tender. Leave to cool slightly.

5 Purée half the soup in small batches in a blender until smooth. Combine the puréed and unpuréed portions, reheat gently, taste and adjust the seasonings.

PEPPERS

Red and yellow peppers are the jewels of vegetarian cookery. One or two of them will add a blaze of color to a stew or casserole, or several of them can be used to make a rich sauce or soup. Peel raw peppers with a swivel-bladed peeler. It's not unlike peeling a carrot or potato, except first, for ease of peeling, the pepper should be cut into its natural sections. The skin of peppers is not very digestible—peeling makes them acceptable to many people who would normally avoid peppers. Also, the cooked pepper pieces are so much more supple and tasty if they have been peeled first. And when peeled peppers are sautéed non-fat style in stock, their juices form a delicious, syrupy sauce.

Celery Root, Cauliflower and Bean Soup with Fennel Seeds

· · · · · · · · · · **Ⓥ** · · **Ⓩ** · · · · · · · · · ·

Makes 5 cups

Celery root is big and ungainly (something like a rutabaga in appearance) with a pleasing, starchy character and a celery-like flavor. Although only half the root is used in this soup, it pays to steam or roast the entire root, or the cut side of the uncooked half will discolor. And there is so much that you can do with a hunk of cooked celery root. Best of all is to purée it and combine it with mashed potatoes. See the section on foil-roasted vegetables (page 136) for more ideas.

I teaspoon fennel seeds	I small cauliflower, separated into
2-3 dry-packed sun-dried tomatoes,	florets and steamed
chopped (use scissors)	1/2 peeled, cooked celery root
1-2 garlic cloves, crushed	(either steamed or roasted, see
6 scallions, sliced	page 140), cubed
pinch of crushed dried chilies	3 tablespoons tomato purée
(or to taste)	I 15-oz can of pinto beans,
2 black olives in brine, drained and	drained and rinsed
flesh slivered off the stones	salt and freshly ground pepper
1/2 cup dry red wine	1-2 tablespoons chopped
4 cups vegetable stock	fresh parsley

1 Put the fennel seeds, sun-dried tomatoes, garlic, onions, dried chili, olive pieces and wine in a large heavy-bottomed saucepan with 1/2 cup of the stock. Cover and bring to the boil, then reduce the heat and simmer for 5-7 minutes or until the garlic and onions are tender and the liquid greatly reduced and syrupy.

2 Add the cauliflower, celery root and another 1/3 cup of the stock to the pan. Stir gently to allow the vegetables to soak up the flavorful liquid.

3 Stir the tomato purée into the remaining stock, and add it to the pan with the beans. Season with salt and pepper, and simmer for 5–6 minutes. Stir in the parsley.

Chunky Grilled Pepper Gazpacho with Tomato Sorbet

· · · · · · · · · · · · **Ⓥ** · · · · · · · · · · · ·

Makes 6 cups

Cold soup is perfect for summer al fresco meals. This bursting-with-summer soup is meant to be served in white china or clear glass (to show off the jewel-like color).

2 28 oz cans of Italian
 tomatoes
4 fresh ripe, flavorful tomatoes,
 peeled and deseeded
finely chopped fresh chile, to taste
1/4 cup balsamic vinegar
 or sherry wine vinegar
1-2 garlic cloves, finely chopped
2 tablespoons chopped fresh
 parsley

2 tablespoons shredded fresh
 mint or basil
4 red peppers (or 2 red peppers
 and 2 yellow peppers), grilled
 and peeled (see page 131),
 deseeded and coarsely chopped
Tomato Sorbet (see page 32),
 optional

1 Drain the canned tomatoes, reserving the juice. Chop the canned and fresh tomatoes.

2 Mix all the ingredients, including the reserved tomato juice, in a large bowl, and chill thoroughly. Serve in shallow bowls or in goblets, with a small scoop of tomato sorbet in the center of each serving.

Tomato Sorbet

· · · · · · · · · · · · **V** · · · · · · · · · · · ·

Makes 2 cups

frozen tomatoes from 2 14-oz
   cans of tomatoes (see note)
juice of I lime

4 tablespoons shredded fresh
   basil or mint
several dashes tabasco sauce

I Put all the ingredients in the bowl of a food processor, and process, stopping to scrape down the sides as necessary, until the mixture forms an icy sorbet consistency.

2 With an ice cream scoop, scoop the icy mixture into balls and serve at once.

N O T E

To freeze canned tomatoes, first drain them very well. Halve the tomatoes, spread them out in one layer on a non-stick baking sheet, and freeze solid. When frozen, gather into a plastic food bag, seal and store in the freezer until needed.

Cold Beet Borscht

· · · · · · · · · · · · · · **Z** · · · · · · · · · · · · · ·

Makes 5 cups

Why are beets not appreciated? When they are available, try this classic sweet and sour chilled Russian soup. Non-fat cottage cheese is a perfect substitute for the usual sour cream. If you have a processor with a shredding or grating attachment, the vegetable preparation will be a snap. It is traditional to set a steaming hot potato right in the center of each bowlful of icy soup, for a "hot as summer, cold as winter" effect.

4 large raw beets,
  peeled and grated
2 large carrots, grated
1 14-oz can of tomatoes
2 leeks, cleaned and chopped
5 cups water

2 tablespoons tomato purée
3 tablespoons lemon juice
2 tablespoons sugar
salt
non-fat cottage cheese and chopped
  fresh dill, to serve

1 Put the beets, carrots, tomatoes and their juice (break up the tomatoes with your fingers), leeks and water in a heavy-bottomed saucepan. Cover and bring to the boil, then reduce the heat and simmer, partially covered, for 45 minutes.

2 Add the tomato purée, lemon juice and sugar, and season with salt. Simmer for a further few minutes. Taste and add more lemon juice, sugar or salt, as necessary. The soup should be tart, but not unpleasantly so.

3 Leave the soup to cool, and then chill. Top each serving with a dollop of cottage cheese and a sprinkling of dill.

V Omit the cottage cheese.

Dips and Spreads

Many of the recipes in this chapter can be surrounded by a profusion of colorful raw vegetable crudités, or non-fat chips (see pages 46-48), and served as a sociable first course or a light lunch. Some make good sandwich spreads and fillings, others work well as garnishes. In fact, you will find these dips and spreads infinitely versatile and suitable for both everyday eating and entertaining.

Mushroom-Apple Pâté

· · · · · · · · · · · · · · (V) · · · · · · · · · · · · · ·

Makes 3 1/2 cups

This pâté is just right spread on small crackers or triangles of toast. Use brown cap mushrooms for a nice, dark color, and don't blend it too smoothly—a slightly rough texture is much more interesting.

1/2 cup dried apple slices,
   cut into pieces
1 cup dry sherry
1/2 cup water
2 lbs brown cap mushrooms, sliced
1-2 garlic cloves, finely chopped

1/2 cup vegetable stock
1-2 dashes teriyaki sauce
1 teaspoon ground coriander
1-2 pinches cayenne
salt and freshly ground pepper

1 Put the apple pieces in a bowl with 1/2 cup of the sherry and the water, and leave to soak.

2 Meanwhile, put the mushrooms, garlic, stock, remaining sherry and teriyaki sauce in a heavy-bottomed frying pan. Bring to a boil, then reduce the heat and simmer briskly, stirring occasionally, until the liquid has almost gone. Add the apples and their soaking liquid, the coriander and cayenne. Simmer, stirring occasionally, until all the liquid has gone. Season with salt and pepper, and leave to cool slightly.

3 Place the mushroom mixture in a food processor and process to a slightly rough purée. Mound the mixture in a bowl, cover and refrigerate until needed.

Duxelles

· · · · · · · · · · · · **V** · · **Z** · · · · · · · · · · · ·

Makes 2 cups

The classic French method for Duxelles—a sort of mushroom hash—calls for finely chopped mushrooms to be sautéed in butter and oil. Substituting my mushroom sauté method, using stock, sherry and soy or teriyaki sauces, works like a dream; it concentrates and enhances the flavor of the mushrooms. Duxelles is a very useful mixture—spread it on toast, or use it to fill filo pastry (see pages 193 and 194) or (for a double mushroom whammy) to fill poached or steamed-roasted mushrooms (see pages 49 and 126).

2 lbs brown cap mushrooms
1 cup vegetable stock
1/2 cup sherry
several dashes teriyaki sauce

6 scallions, chopped
1 teaspoon dried tarragon, crumbled
salt and freshly ground pepper

1 Quarter the mushrooms and put them in a food processor. "Pulse" the machine on and off quickly until the mushrooms are very finely chopped. You will need to do this in two or more batches.

2 Empty all the chopped mushrooms into a deep, heavy-bottomed frying pan. Add the stock, sherry, teriyaki sauce, scallions and tarragon, and stir well. (The mushrooms will be barely moistened but it doesn't matter.)

3 Cook over moderate heat, stirring occasionally, until the mushrooms have rendered quite a bit of liquid. Increase the heat slightly and simmer briskly, stirring occasionally, until the mushrooms are very dark, very thick and quite dry. Reduce the heat as the liquid cooks away, to minimize scorching. Season with salt and pepper. Spoon into a bowl, cool, cover and store in the refrigerator until needed.

Green Pea Dip

· · · · · · · · · · · · · · V · · · · · · · · · · · · ·

Makes 2 cups

Frozen peas, like frozen corn, are handy to have in the freezer at all times. If you have a microwave, they can be thawed and ready to go in minutes. Both vegetables take to the freezing process very well. This dip has a vividly fresh character—to call it "garden-fresh" is to lapse into cliché, but I could hardly describe it any other way, even if it has been harvested from the freezer! I often use this as a kind of substitute guacamole (Mexican avocado spread). If you want to give it a slightly more Mexican character, add some ground cumin and chopped fresh cilantro.

juice of 1 lime
1 fresh chile pepper, deseeded
   and chopped
4 tablespoons chopped fresh parsley

1 lb thawed frozen peas
3-4 scallions, chopped
salt

1 Place all the ingredients, except the scallions and salt, in a blender or food processor, and process until coarsely chopped.

2 Add the onions, season with salt, and process to a rough purée. Spoon into a bowl, cover and refrigerate until needed.

Roasted Vegetable Dip

· · · · · · · · · · · · **Ⓥ** · · · · · · · · · · · ·

Makes 2 cups

Spread this deeply flavored purée on bread, scoop it up with lettuce leaves or, if you can't wait to dive in, eat it with a spoon. It's the roasting (especially of the garlic) and the smokiness of the grilled peppers that give the purée its depth. Roasting garlic in this manner renders the bulb mellow and sweet: one clove of raw garlic, pushed through a garlic press, is actually stronger than an entire roasted bulb.

2 medium eggplants, about
   8 oz each
I large, firm head of garlic
2 red peppers, grilled and peeled
   (see page 131), then diced
I large ripe tomato, peeled,
   deseeded and chopped
   (or, out of season, use 2-3
   canned Italian tomatoes,
   drained and chopped)

juice of 1/2 lemon
4 scallions, cut in half
   lengthwise and sliced across thinly
6 tablespoons chopped fresh parsley
3 tablespoons chopped fresh
   mint or basil
salt and freshly ground pepper

I Preheat the oven to 375°F.

2 Prick the eggplants in several places with a fork or thin skewer. Remove the papery outer covering of the garlic, but do not separate the head into cloves. Wrap the garlic in foil. Bake both eggplant and garlic directly in the oven for 45-55 minutes or until the eggplant is soft and collapsed, and the garlic feels soft within its skin. Leave to cool on a wire rack.

3 When both the eggplant and garlic are cool enough to handle, trim the stems from the eggplant and strip off the skin. Roughly chop the flesh and put in a bowl. Separate the garlic cloves, and squeeze each clove over the bowl so that the puréed garlic pops out (in fact, it *oozes* out, just like toothpaste from a tube).

4 Add the remaining ingredients to the bowl. With an electric mixer, beat the mixture into a rough purée, or pulse on and off in a food processor. Taste and adjust the seasoning, adding more salt, pepper and lemon juice as needed. Cover and chill for at least 1 hour before serving.

Mellow Garlic and Lentil Spread

· · · · · · · · · · · · · Ⓥ · · · · · · · · · · · · · ·

Makes 2 cups

Red lentils need no soaking, cook quickly, and can be used to make a lovely spread for bread. Three versions follow; the first features mild garlic, the second has an Italian accent, and the third combines lemon juice with a lively spice mixture.

I cup split red lentils, rinsed	I-2 dashes teriyaki sauce
3 garlic cloves, halved	a few drops tabasco sauce
2 cups vegetable stock or water	1/4 teaspoon Dijon mustard
salt and freshly ground pepper	vegetable bouillon powder
	(optional)

I Put the lentils, garlic and stock or water in a heavy-bottomed saucepan. Bring to the boil, then reduce the heat and simmer, uncovered, for 20-30 minutes or until the lentils are tender. Skim off foam from the surface from time to time, and add more liquid if needed to prevent scorching.

2 Season the mixture with the remaining ingredients (adding some vegetable bouillon powder if you have used water instead of stock), and simmer gently for a few more minutes until the lentils are a thick purée. Leave to cool.

3 Purée the mixture in a blender or food processor until smooth, then transfer to a bowl, cover and store in the refrigerator until needed.

Olive-Sun-dried Tomato-Lentil Spread

· · · · · · · · · · · · · **V** · · · · · · · · · · · · ·

Makes 2 cups

An infusion of scallions, sun-dried tomatoes, garlic, olives and chilies is one of my favorite flavor-bases. It adds a lively and delicate richness to split red lentil, just the thing for spreading on vegetables and crusty bread.

3 small scallions, sliced
2 dry-packed sun-dried
  tomatoes, chopped
  (use scissors)
I garlic clove, crushed
2-3 black olives in brine, drained
  and flesh slivered off the stones
pinch of crushed dried chilies

I/2 cup vegetable stock
I cup split red lentils, rinsed
2 cups vegetable stock or water
vegetable bouillon powder
  (optional)

I Put the onions, tomatoes, garlic, olive slivers and chili in a heavy-bottomed saucepan with the 1/2 cup of stock. Bring to a boil, then reduce the heat and simmer briskly for a few minutes or until the onions are very tender and the liquid almost gone.

2 Stir in the red lentils and the salt-free stock or water. Simmer for 20-30 minutes or until the lentils are tender, adding more liquid if needed to prevent scorching. Season with salt and pepper (and add some vegetable bouillon powder if you have used water instead of stock) and simmer gently for a few more minutes until the lentils are a thick purée. Leave to cool.

3 Purée the mixture in a blender or food processor until smooth, then transfer to a bowl, cover and store in the refrigerator until needed.

Middle-Eastern Lentil Spread

· · · · · · · · · · · · **V** · · · · · · · · · · · ·

Makes 2 cups

Lemon, cumin and coriander work well with red lentils. This version of lentil spread is particularly good as a dip with pita crisps (see page 46).

(see page 46)

1/2 cup vegetable stock
juice of 1/2 lemon
3/4 teaspoon ground cumin
3/4 teaspoon ground coriander
pinch of cayenne
3-4 scallions, sliced
1-2 garlic cloves, crushed

1 cup split red lentils, rinsed
about 2 cups vegetable stock
 or water
salt and freshly ground pepper
vegetable bouillon powder
 (optional)

1 Pour the 1/2 cup of stock into a heavy-bottomed saucepan, and add the lemon juice, spices, scallions and garlic. Bring to a boil, then reduce the heat and simmer for a few minutes until the onions are tender and the liquid almost gone.

2 Stir in the red lentils and the salt-free stock or water, and simmer for 20-30 minutes or until the lentils are tender. Add more liquid, if necessary, to prevent scorching. Season with salt and pepper (adding some vegetable bouillon powder if you have used water instead of stock), and simmer gently for a few more minutes until the lentils are a thick purée. Leave to cool.

3 Purée the mixture in a blender or food processor until smooth, then transfer to a bowl, cover and store in the refrigerator until needed.

Spicy Bean Dip

· · · · · · · · · · · **Ⓥ** · · **Ⓩ** · · · · · · · · · · ·

Makes 3 cups

A can of beans, tomatoes and a bold hand with the seasonings give you a most delicious pot of beans. Purée them (as described in step 3) and eat, still warm, with vegetable dippers, or any of the crisps at the end of this chapter (see pages 46-48). Alternatively, purée only half of the mixture then mix with the unpuréed portion and wrap in wheat tortillas, garnished with Green Pea Dip (see page 37) and Creamy Herb Sauce (see page 192). Or dilute the half-puréed, half-unpuréed version with vegetable stock and serve as a soup. Or prepare only as far as step 2, and serve on toast. Or…but I'm sure you will come up with plenty of your own ideas.

12 scallions, sliced
3-4 garlic cloves, cut into chunks
3-4 dry-packed, sun-dried tomatoes,
   chopped (use scissors) (optional)
1 cup vegetable stock
1/2 cup dry white vermouth
1-2 generous pinches of
   ground cumin
1-2 generous pinches of crushed
   dried chilies
2 15-oz cans of beans
   (cannellini, pinto or red kidney),
   drained and rinsed

1 14-oz can of chopped tomatoes,
   puréed in the blender with
   3 tablespoons tomato paste
salt and freshly ground pepper
2 tablespoons chopped
   fresh parsley
1-2 tablespoons chopped fresh
   cilantro, shredded fresh mint
   or shredded fresh basil
juice of 1/2 lime

1 Put the onions, garlic, sun-dried tomatoes (if using), stock, vermouth, cumin and chile in a heavy-bottomed saucepan. Cover and boil for 5-7 minutes. Uncover and simmer briskly, stirring occasionally, until the liquid is reduced and syrupy, and the garlic meltingly tender.

2 Add the beans and stir to coat them with the onion-spice mixture. Stir in the chopped tomato mixture and season with salt and pepper. Simmer, uncovered, for about 15 minutes or until thick. Stir in the chopped herbs and the lime juice. Leave to cool slightly.

3 Process the mixture to a rough purée in a blender or food processor, then transfer to a bowl and serve warm.

Cannellini-Red Pepper Dip

Makes 2 cups

More wonderful convenience food: canned cannellini (white kidney) beans and bottled or canned red peppers. They team up to make a beautifully blushing, compellingly creamy spread or dip. Dilute it with stock, add some chopped herbs, and it makes a quick and easy sauce for pasta or grains.

1 15-oz can of cannellini beans	a good pinch of dried chile flakes
1 15-oz can or jar of red peppers	4-5 dry-packed, sun-dried tomatoes,
1/4 teaspoon cumin seeds	diced (with scissors) (optional)
3 garlic cloves, crushed	1 cup vegetable stock
	salt and freshly ground pepper

1 Empty the beans and the peppers into a colander. Rinse under cold running water and set aside to drain well.

2 Put the cumin seeds in a frying pan and heat gently for about 1 minute or until toasted and fragrant, stirring constantly. Add the garlic, chile, tomatoes (if using) and stock. Cover and boil for 3-4 minutes. Uncover and simmer until the garlic is tender and the liquid has reduced considerably and become syrupy.

3 Put the drained peppers and beans in a food processor, and scrape in the garlic-chile infusion. Season with salt and pepper, then purée until smooth. Transfer to a bowl, cover and refrigerate until needed.

Hummus

· · · · · · · · · · · · · **ⓥ** · · · · · · · · · · · · ·

Makes 2 cups

Hummus (chickpea spread) is usually made with tahini (sesame seed paste) and raw garlic, in addition to the basic chickpea purée. Sesame seeds are a high-fat food—in tahini they are concentrated. Some recipes for hummus call for olive oil as well, so all in all, it can be a wickedly fattening dish. I use 1/2 tablespoon sesame seeds and stock-sautéed garlic in place of the more traditional raw garlic-tahini-olive oil mixture. The 1/2 tablespoon seeds adds just 2 grams of fat to the recipe (as opposed to the 28 grams of fat in 4 tablespoons tahini), and the stock-sautéed garlic adds a much gentler garlic flavor than raw garlic would. Add lemon juice to your taste—some like a very lemony hummus, others don't.

1/2 tablespoon sesame seeds	1/2 cup vegetable stock
juice of 1 1/2-2 lemons	2 15-oz cans of chickpeas
2 garlic cloves, crushed	(also known as garbonzo beans)

1 Put the sesame seeds in a heavy-bottomed frying pan, and heat gently for about 1 minute or until toasted and fragrant, stirring constantly.

2 Stir in the juice of 1/2 lemon, the garlic and stock, and bring to a boil. Cook, stirring, until the garlic is tender and the liquid almost gone.

3 Drain the chickpeas, reserving their liquid. Put the sesame mixture in a blender or food processor, and add a quarter of the chickpea liquid. Process for a few moments, then add a quarter of the chickpeas and process until smooth.

4 Add the juice of 1 lemon and the remaining chickpeas. Process until the hummus has the delightful consistency of fluffy mashed potatoes. Taste, add more lemon juice if required, and process once more. Transfer to a bowl, cover and refrigerate until needed.

Yogurt "Cream" Cheese

· ·

Low-fat yogurt can be thin and watery. Remedy this by draining it overnight. The whey seeps away, leaving a thick, creamy, spreadable cheese. Instead of herbs, try crushed garlic marinated in a bit of white wine (or balsamic) vinegar. Or try a sweet spread—fold in a bit of honey or marmalade. This "cheese" is delicious spread on bagels or toast and is excellent in sandwiches.

low-fat yogurt   chopped fresh herbs

1 Line a sieve with a double layer of muslin. Place over a large bowl. Pour the yogurt into the sieve, fold the cloth over the top and refrigerate overnight.

2 Next day, drain the liquid from the bowl, and rinse and dry the bowl. Scrape the drained yogurt into the bowl and fold in the herbs. Cover and refrigerate until needed.

Beet-Chutney Dip

· · · · · · · · · · **V** · · · · · · · · · · · · ·

Makes 1 cup

If you crave edible fire, and you can find Tuscan lemon chutney or lime-chili chutney, try them in this recipe in place of mango chutney. Hot mango chutney is good, too, of course, but it will just tingle on the tongue—it won't try to blow the top of your head off. On the other hand, if your palate is not part-asbestos, use ordinary mango chutney in place of the hot version.

1 cup chunked cooked   2-3 tablespoons hot (spicy)
  beets (with no vinegar)   mango chutney

1 Cut the beet into chunks and put in a blender or food processor with the chutney. Process to a rough purée.

2 Transfer to a bowl, cover and store in the fridge until needed.

· · · **45** · · ·

Dippers

The next three recipes make non-fat dippers for all your dips and spreads. Store-bought potato-chips, tortilla chips, etc., pile on the fat calories; making your own is easy and fun. Every oven is different, so take the timing given as a very general guide only, and the first time you make these, check them carefully—they might need more or less time.

Pita Crisps

· · · · · · · · · · · · **V** · · · · · · · · · · · ·

brown or white pita bread

1 Preheat the oven to 300°F.

2 With kitchen scissors, cut the pita bread into quarters or eighths, then separate each piece into two. Arrange in one layer on a nonstick baking sheet, and bake in the oven for 10-15 minutes or until dried out and crisp. They will keep for several weeks in an airtight container.

Tortilla Chips

· · · · · · · · · · · · · · (V) · · · · · · · · · · · · · ·

Corn tortillas are a wonderfully versatile and delicious Mexican food. They resemble wheat chapattis, but are made from corn meal, and contain no fat whatsoever.

corn tortillas

1 Preheat the oven to 300°F.

2 Bake the tortillas directly in the oven for 15-20 minutes, turning once, until crisp right through (they will break with a clean snap). Break into quarters or eighths, cool and store in an airtight container (they will keep for a month or more).

MICROWAVE METHOD

1 Put a double layer of paper towels on the microwave turntable.

2 Arrange five tortillas on the paper around the outside of the turntable. They should not quite touch each other. Microwave on high (100%) for 2-2 1/2 minutes.

3 If the towels are wet, replace them. Turn the tortillas over and microwave on high (100%) for another 2-2 1/2 minutes.

4 Place the tortillas on a wire rack and let rest for 5 minutes. Break into quarters or eighths, cool and store in an airtight container.

Potato Chips

· · · · · · · · · · · · **V** · · · · · · · · · · ·

Makes about 20 chips

Home-made potato chips? Why not? Think of the luxury—pure potato, minimal grease. What bliss!

I large baking potato

oil and water spray (see page 5)
salt (optional)

I Preheat the oven to 350°F.

2 Slice the potato paper-thin, using the slicing disk of a food processor, or the slicing slot on an old-fashioned grater.

3 Arrange the slices in a single layer on two non-stick baking sheets that you have misted lightly with oil spray. Salt lightly, if desired. Bake in the oven for about 15 minutes. Reposition the chips on the sheets, and reposition the sheets in the oven, if necessary, to ensure even browning, and bake for another 3-5 minutes or until the potato slices are crisp and browned, but not burnt.

Poached Mushrooms
for Stuffing or Dipping

· · · · · · · · · · **V** · · **Z** · · · · · · · · ·

A platter of chicory leaves, red, yellow and green peppers (trimmed and cut into little boats), and these mushroom caps, all filled with a colorful variety of dips and spreads, makes an arresting edible display for a buffet table. As a design statement they only have a moment of glory; when the hungry hordes attack, the platter empties very quickly. If you don't feel like stuffing all those little morsels, put a selection of colorful dips and spreads into pretty bowls. Place on a large platter, and surround with heaps of chicory leaves, pepper boats and mushroom caps.

about 1 lb firm, white,
   medium-sized or
   button mushrooms
1/2 cup vegetable stock

about 1/2 cup dry sherry
1-2 dashes teriyaki sauce

1 Carefully remove the stems from the mushroom caps. Save the stems for another use (Duxelles or Mushroom Ragout, see pages 36 and 167, for instance). With a teaspoon, gently even out the mushroom cap opening so it will hold a filling nicely.

2 Pour the stock, sherry and teriyaki sauce into a non-stick frying pan that will hold the mushroom caps in one layer. Bring the liquid to the boil, add the mushroom caps in one layer, open sides up, reduce the heat, cover and simmer for 2-3 minutes. Uncover, raise the heat and cook, tossing the mushrooms in the pan, for a minute or so or until the caps are cooked but still quite firm, and the liquid is reduced and syrupy. Remove the mushroom caps from the pan, and drain upside down on paper towels. Allow to cool before stuffing.

Grains

Complex carbohydrate, fat-soluble vitamins, fiber, protein, essential fatty acids—grains have them all. Combined with beans, grains form a high-quality protein, which is why old favorites from around the world, like tortillas and beans, minestrone soup (with macaroni and beans), red beans and rice, black beans and rice, baked beans on toast, and so on nourish entire populations. Although these classics combine beans and grains in the same meal, it is not necessary always to eat them together. If you eat beans and grains frequently, their protein will complement each other even if they are consumed at different times of the day.

The most familiar grains are rice and wheat (in the form of pasta, bread and breakfast cereals), but there is a world of additional choices. Check out your supermarket and the health food store, and cast your eyes over the bounty: buckwheat, millet, couscous, cracked wheat, wild rice (the most luxurious grain of all). What feasting lies in store! Keep this in mind: the less processing, the more nutrition, so whenever possible, choose the whole grain.

SERVING NOTE

I find the easiest way to measure grains, cooked or raw, is with a measuring cup. One-half to 1 cup cooked grain constitutes a side dish serving, 2 1/2 to 3 cups, a main dish serving. As always, be flexible: one person's satisfying meal is another's tantalizing taste, and yet another's painful over-indulgence!

As far as pasta is concerned, conventional wisdom advises 1/8 lb. (raw weight) pasta per serving, but I find this totally absurd. For a main course, 1/4 to 1/2 lb. is more like it, but, as always, use your appetite as a guide.

Rice

Brown rice bursts with nutrients and has a superb taste and texture: nutty, chewy, not to mention deeply comforting and satisfying. I think cooked brown rice makes a wonderful breakfast: mix in a handful of raisins or chopped dried fruit (try dried mango—what a treat!) and pour some warm skim milk over it into which you have mixed some skim-milk powder for extra richness and nutrition.

To cook brown rice (both short- and long-grain)

Rice will expand to three times its volume when cooked. Measure the uncooked rice by pouring it into a measuring cup: 1 cup rice will yield 3 cups cooked rice. Choose a heavy-bottomed saucepan (with room for the rice to expand) that can be covered tightly. Measure the rice first, then rinse it in a sieve under cold running water. Pour the rice into the pan, then pour in twice the volume of stock or water. In other words, for 1 cup raw rice, add 2 cups liquid. Add some salt and a bay leaf, and bring to a boil. Stir once, cover tightly, reduce the heat, and simmer over very low heat for 45-55 minutes for long grain, 35-40 minutes for short-grain. (The exact timing depends on the rice, your stove, and the thickness of the pan.) Uncover, fluff with a fork, drape with a clean tea-towel, re-cover over the teatowel, and leave, off the heat, for 10 minutes. The rice will be tender and fluffy, and the liquid absorbed.

Pan-Fried Wild Rice Fritters

. . . .

Makes 6

Leftover wild rice is a gastronomic treasure. It always pays to make too much (although you may have to hide it to ensure that there are leftovers). I love these hot fritters for breakfast, or serve them in an overlapping circle surrounding a vegetable stew or a heap of spicy beans.

1 cup cooked wild rice
  (see page 54)
2 egg whites, lightly beaten

olive oil and water spray
  (see page 5)

1 Stir the wild rice into the lightly beaten egg white.

2 Mist a non-stick frying pan with the oil spray and heat. Drop the wild rice mixture, in rounded tablespoonfuls, into the pan, and flatten with a broad spatula. Pan-fry until set on one side, then slide the spatula beneath each fritter to loosen, and carefully turn them over. Cook on the second side until both sides are crisp and golden. Transfer to a warm plate; tent loosely with foil to keep warm. Repeat until the rice mixture is used, making about six fritters.

Pan-Fried Brown Rice Fritters

· ·

Makes 6

Good enough reason to keep cooked rice on hand, these adorable little frit-
ters are pan-fried in a non-stick frying pan with a bare misting of oil.

1 1/2 cups cooked short-grain
   brown rice (see page 51)
2 egg whites, lightly beaten
salt and freshly ground pepper

1-1 1/2 tablespoons grated
   Parmesan cheese
olive oil and water spray
   (see page 5)

1 Stir the rice into the lightly beaten egg white and season with salt
and pepper. Toss with two spoons to combine thoroughly, and to
break up any clumps of rice. Stir in the cheese.

2 Mist a non-stick frying pan with the oil spray and heat. Drop the
rice mixture in rounded tablespoonfuls into the pan, and flatten with
a broad spatula. Pan-fry until completely set on one side, then carefully slide the spatula under to loosen and flip over the fritters. Pan-fry
until cooked through and golden on both sides. Transfer to a warm
plate and tent loosely with foil to keep warm while making remaining
fritters. Repeat until the rice batter is used, making about six fritters.

Wild Rice Pilaf

. . . .

Makes 3 cups

Wild rice is not a rice at all, but a native American aquatic wild grass, Zizania aquatica. Although wild rice is now cultivated in California, at one time the truly wild variety was the only one available. The really wild stuff grows in abundance in parts of Minnesota and Wisconsin, and is gathered there with laborious care by Native Americans. They canoe down the narrow watery paths that meander through the tall grain, flailing away at the stalks, until the canoe is full of the precious seeds. Centuries ago, the Ojibway Indians called it mahnomen (good grain) and the early French explorers of the New World called it folle avoine (crazy oat).

Cook wild rice grains until they begin to puff open. Some of the grains will remain closed; it is the contrast between the two that gives a dish of wild rice such wonderful texture. Be sure not to overcook it, however— some of the grains should remain al dente to be interesting. During the cooking, be prepared to be flexible; some batches cook quicker than others. Wild rice is available from health food stores, specialty stores and some supermakets.

3 cups vegetable stock	1/4 teaspoon chopped fresh
2 carrots, finely chopped	thyme or a pinch of dried thyme
5 scallions, thinly sliced	1 bay leaf
1 cup raw wild rice	salt and freshly ground pepper

1 Preheat the oven to 350°F.

2 Put 1 cup of the stock in a flameproof casserole that can be covered. Add the carrots and scallions and bring to a boil. Reduce the heat, cover and simmer until the vegetables are tender and the liquid almost gone. Add the wild rice and stir so that the vegetables and rice are well combined. Add the remaining stock and the herbs, and season with salt and pepper. Bring back to a boil, then cover and bake in the oven for 45-55 minutes or until all the liquid is absorbed, and the wild rice cooked (it should remain somewhat crunchy). Remove from the oven, lift off the lid and drape a clean tea-towel over the open pan. Replace the lid over the towel and leave for 5-10 minutes. Remove the bay leaf before serving.

Rice with Scallions and Vermouth

. . . .

Makes 2 cups

This is a kind of instant risotto—it's ridiculously easy to make (if you have the cooked rice on hand) and, as with most rice dishes, it is extremely comforting. Make it into a complete meal by stirring in some stir-fried or steamed asparagus tips, some lightly cooked fresh or frozen peas and some chopped fresh herbs.

1/2 cup dry white vermouth
1/2 cup vegetable stock
6 scallions, sliced
2 cups cooked short-grain
    brown rice (see page 51)

salt and freshly ground pepper
2-3 tablespoons grated
    Parmesan cheese (optional)

1 Put the vermouth, stock and scallions in a frying pan. Bring to a boil, then reduce the heat and simmer until the liquid is reduced by half.

2 Stir in the rice, season with salt and pepper, and cook, stirring, over gentle heat until the rice is soft and thoroughly hot. Serve at once or, if you wish, sprinkle in the cheese, stir and cook over the lowest heat until the cheese has melted into the rice.

Ⓥ Omit the Parmesan.

Spinach-Rice Pie

. . . .

Serves 4–6

Add mozzarella cheese to a rice crust mixture to make a pie crust and then fill the baked crust with vividly flavored spinach for a glorious main dish. The recipe below makes more spinach than you need to fill the crust. It's so good, you may find that you've polished it off all by yourself as you prepare the meal; if not, use it to fill filo rolls or triangles (see page 195), serve it as a side vegetable at another meal, or cook it in a frittata (see page 178).

BASE
2 cups well-seasoned cooked
   short-grain brown rice
   (see page 51)
2 egg whites, lightly beaten
1/4 lb. low-fat mozzarella cheese,
   shredded
olive oil and water spray
   (see page 5)

FILLING
1 bag (about 2 lbs)
   frozen chopped spinach, thawed

6 scallions, sliced
2-3 dry-packed sun-dried tomatoes,
   chopped (use scissors)
3 black olives in brine, drained and
   flesh slivered off the stones
1-2 garlic cloves, crushed
1 cup vegetable stock
salt and freshly ground pepper
1 tablespoon tomato purée
5 tablespoons grated Parmesan
   cheese

1 Preheat the oven to 425°F.

2 Put the rice, egg white and mozzarella cheese in a bowl. Toss with two spoons to mix thoroughly and to break up any clumps of rice. Mist an 11-inch non-stick flat-bottomed pan with the oil spray, and tip the rice into the dish. Use the back of a large spoon to spread it evenly over the bottom and up the sides of the dish. Bake for 20 minutes.

3 Meanwhile, drain the spinach in a colander and squeeze it as dry as possible. Set aside.

4 Put the scallions, sun-dried tomatoes, olives, garlic and stock in a frying pan. Bring to a boil, then reduce the heat and simmer until the onions are tender and the liquid almost gone. Stir in the spinach and season well with salt and pepper. Stir and cook for a few minutes or until the spinach is hot and cooked. (It won't take long so take care not to overcook.) Stir in the tomato purée and 2 tablespoons of the Parmesan cheese.

5 Spread the spinach mixture in the cooked rice crust. (You will have more than you need; save the rest for another meal.) Sprinkle evenly with the remaining Parmesan cheese, then broil for 2-3 minutes or until the cheese is melted and bubbly.

VARIATION

Rice "Pizza"

Spread the rice crust with warm tomato sauce (see page 91), sprinkle with shredded low-fat mozzarella, and broil until the cheese melts. The crust under the sauce softens up, but the surrounding edges become crunchy and the melted cheese adds a creamy dimension. It is a most seductive combination.

Mushroom Pie

· ·

Serves 6

A mixture of cooked brown rice and lightly beaten egg white can be used to line a flan dish and baked to form a nutritious and delicious pie crust. The rice crust can be filled with almost any savory mixture: here I've used a creamy mushroom ragout.

2 egg whites
1/2 tablespoon Dijon mustard
4 cups well-seasoned cooked
   brown rice (see page 51)

oil and water spray (see page 5)
Creamy Mushroom Ragout
   (see page 167), warmed

1 Preheat the oven to 425°F.

2 Lightly beat the egg whites with the mustard. Stir in the rice, and toss with two spoons to combine well and to break up any clumps of rice. Mist a non-stick 11-inch flat-bottomed pan with the oil spray, and scrape the rice mixture into the dish. With the back of a large spoon, press the rice over the bottom and up the sides of the dish. Bake in the oven for 20 minutes.

3 Spoon the Mushroom Ragout into the rice crust and serve at once.

Rice and Grilled Vegetable Pie

. . . .

Serves 4–6

Based on a traditional Italian recipe, this pie is much leaner than the orig-
inal, although it retains the characteristic flavor and appearance. A wedge
of this and a salad make an incomparable evening meal. It's good warm
or at room temperature (or straight out of the fridge—I know!).

Olive oil and water spray
  (see page 5)
4 tablespoons breadcrumbs
5 tablespoons grated Parmesan
  cheese
4 cups cooked brown rice
  (see page 51)

2 cups tomato sauce
  (see pages 91 and 92)
2 eggplants, sliced and grilled
  (see page 129)
5 zucchini, sliced and grilled
  (see page 130)

1 Preheat the oven to 425°F.

2 Mist an 11-inch non-stick flan tin with oil spray. Mix the breadcrumbs with 2 tablespoons of the Parmesan cheese. Spoon this mixture into the tin, and shake the tin to spread the crumbs all over the
bottom. Tilt the tin so the crumbs coat the sides.

3 Mix the rice with the tomato sauce and the remaining cheese.
Spread half this mixture over the bottom and up the sides of the flan
tin. Arrange the grilled vegetables, in one overlapping layer of slices,
on the rice base, then spread the remaining rice mixture over the vegetables. Sprinkle evenly with the remaining breadcrumb mixture. Mist
the top very lightly with the olive oil spray.

4 Bake in the oven for 20-30 minutes or until the top is golden
brown, and the pie is slightly puffy and bubbly. Remove from the oven
and leave on a rack for 5-10 minutes before cutting into wedges.

Sweet Rice Pulao

· · · · · · · · · · · · ⓥ · · · · · · · · · · · ·

Makes 3 cups

This is the perfect partner for the vegetable curries on pages 156-62, along with Raita (see pages 191-92) and Green Split Pea Dhal (see page 113). Arrange it all on a large white platter to show it off. Color, texture, flavor, temperature contrast—all the things I love in a meal—leap off the platter.

3 cups vegetable stock
juice of 1/2 lemon and 1/2 orange
1/2-inch piece of fresh ginger,
    peeled and crushed
1 red or yellow pepper, peeled,
   deseeded and chopped
2 small onions, chopped
2 carrots, chopped
1/4 teaspoon each of ground
    cinnamon, ground coriander
    and ground turmeric

1 small bay leaf
1/8 teaspoon ground allspice
two 14-oz cans of tomatoes,
    drained, deseeded and chopped
2 tablespoons raisins
2 tablespoons chopped
    dried apricots
1 cup raw long-grain
    brown rice
salt and freshly ground pepper

1 Put 1 cup of the stock, the fruit juices, ginger, vegetables and spices in a flameproof casserole or heavy-bottomed saucepan. Bring to a boil, cover, reduce the heat and simmer for 5 minutes. Uncover and simmer for 3-5 minutes more or until the vegetables are tender and the liquid almost gone. Stir in the tomatoes and dried fruits, and simmer, stirring, for a few minutes or until the mixture has thickened.

2 Add the rice and stir to combine well. Stir in the remaining stock, season liberally with salt and pepper, and bring to a boil. Reduce the heat, cover the pan and simmer very gently for 40-45 minutes. Remove from the heat. Uncover and fluff up the rice with a fork. Drape a clean tea-towel over the open pan, replace the lid over the tea-towel, and leave to stand for 5-10 minutes. Remove and discard the bay leaf before serving.

Molded Rice Pulao with Stir-Fried Peppers

· · · · · · · · · · · · **ⓥ** · · · · · · · · · · · ·

Serves 6

Mold the colorful rice in a teacup, then unmold it onto a pretty plate. Surround with stir-fried peppers for a knock-out dinner party accompaniment.

warm Sweet Rice Pulao
  (see page 60)
2 red peppers
2 yellow peppers
1 cup vegetable stock
good pinch of ground cumin

good pinch of ground coriander
salt and freshly ground pepper
lemon or lime and orange wedges,
  chopped fresh parsley and
  chopped fresh cilantro, to serve

1 Pack the warm rice pulao into teacups, cover with plastic wrap and set aside.

2 Halve the peppers and remove their stems, seeds and ribs. Cut the peppers lengthways into their natural sections, and peel them with a swivel-bladed vegetable peeler. Cut the sections into 1/2-inch-wide strips.

3 Put the pepper strips in a frying pan, add the stock, and season with the spices, salt and pepper. Bring to the boil, then reduce the heat and simmer briskly, stirring frequently, until the peppers are tender and bathed in a syrupy glaze.

4 To serve, unmold the rice onto individual plates. (To do this, remove the plastic wrap, put a plate over a teacup, turn over, give it a good shake and the molded rice will slide out.) Surround each mound of rice with a wreath of warm or cold peppers, add 2-3 small wedges of lemon or lime and orange, and sprinkle chopped herbs over the rice mounds.

Brown Rice Salad
with Cauliflower

. . . .

Makes 5 cups

*The ivory of the cauliflower and the dressing and the brown of the rice
make for a rather muted appearance, but the garnish of Cherry Tomato
and Cucumber Relish and chopped herbs adds a jolt of color. If you wish,
use halved cherry tomatoes in plate of the relish.*

1/4 cup balsamic vinegar
juice of I large lemon
I teaspoon sugar
2-3 dashes teriyaki sauce
2 cups warm, cooked long-grain
   brown rice (see page 51)
I small cauliflower,
   separated into florets
   and steamed
salt and freshly ground pepper

3 tablespoons non-fat cottage cheese
2 tablespoons low-fat
   mayonnaise-style dressing
I 1/2 teaspoons Dijon mustard
1-2 tablespoons snipped fresh chives
1-2 tablespoons chopped
   fresh parsley
Cherry Tomato and Cucumber
   Relish (see page 188), to serve

1 Mix the vinegar, lemon juice, sugar and teriyaki sauce, and add to
the rice. Toss with two spoons to coat the rice thoroughly, and to
break up any clumps of rice. Toss in the cauliflower, and season with
salt and pepper.

2 Whisk together the cottage cheese, mayonnaise and Dijon mustard.
Fold this mixture into the rice and cauliflower, then fold in the herbs.
To serve, arrange on a platter, and surround with Cherry Tomato and
Cucumber Relish.

Smoked Tofu Kedgeree

. . . .

Makes 4 cups

Here, sto.............. .... butter, and smoked tofu for haddock, to make a stunning dish. ....tle smokiness of the tofu and spiciness of the garam masala work well together. Of all the available beans, soybeans have the most (and the highest-quality) protein. They also have the highest fat content but are still a comparatively low-fat food. Tofu is, essentially, soybean cheese; it is made from curdled soy milk. The blandness of tofu and its slightly spongy texture mean that it soaks up the flavors of infusions and dressings extremely well.

1 cup vegetable stock	1 cup frozen peas
3 red peppers, peeled, deseeded and chopped	1 cup cooked long-grain brown rice (see page 51)
2 tablespoons skim-milk powder	1/2 lb. smoked tofu, cut into 1-inch cubes
1/2 cup skim milk	salt and freshly ground pepper
1 tablespoon garam masala	chopped fresh parsley, to serve
1 cup frozen corn	

1 Put the stock and peppers in a large, heavy-bottomed frying pan. Bring to a boil, then reduce the heat and simmer until the peppers are tender and the liquid greatly reduced and syrupy. Mix the skim-milk powder into the milk, and stir into the peppers with the garam masala. Simmer very gently for 1-2 minutes, stirring.

2 Add the vegetables to the pan, and cook for a few minutes, stirring, until the vegetables are warmed through and cooked. Add the rice, and stir until everything is well combined.

3 Add the tofu, and season with salt and pepper. Cook, stirring gently for a few moments (be careful not to break up the tofu) until heated through. Serve, sprinkled with parsley.

Brown Rice Salad
with Broccoli

· · · · · · · · · · · **Ⓥ** · · · · · · · · · ·

Makes 5 cups

Here, rice and broccoli are dressed with an Oriental-style mixture of citrus juice, teriyaki and sugar, with a little balsamic vinegar to jazz it up. If you dress the rice while it is still warm, the flavors soak in most efficiently.

I lb broccoli
4 cups warm, cooked
   long-grain brown rice
   (see page 51)
cherry tomatoes, halved, and
   fresh cilantro leaves, to serve

DRESSING
juice of 3 large oranges
juice of 3 limes
3 tablespoons teriyaki sauce
2 tablespoons balsamic vinegar
3 teaspoons sugar
1/2-inch piece of ginger,
   peeled and crushed
I garlic clove, crushed

I Whisk all the dressing ingredients together in a small bowl, and set aside.

2 Cut the florets from the broccoli and put them in a steamer basket. Cut off and discard the tough woody bottoms of the stalks, peel the stalks, and quarter them lengthwise. Add the stalks to the steamer basket. Steam over boiling water for about 10 minutes or until "crisp-tender"—in other words, it should still have a bit of a crunch and remain bright green. Rinse under cold running water to set the color, drain well, and set aside to cool.

3 Put the rice in a large bowl and pour over half the dressing. Toss with two spoons to mix well, and to break up any clumps of rice. Toss the cooled broccoli with the remaining dressing, then gently fold the broccoli into the rice. Serve spread out on a platter, surrounded by halved cherry tomatoes and sprinkled with cilantro leaves.

Bulgur

Tabouli

· · · · · · · · · · · · · **V** · · · · · · · · · · · ·

Makes 5 cups

Tabouli is a refreshing and colorful salad of herbs, tomatoes and grain (bulgur wheat). The success of the dish depends on the tomatoes; they must he ripe and bursting with flavor. If you can't find large, tasty tomatoes, this salad will also work with halved cherry tomatoes.

1/2 lb bulgur wheat
1/2 cup lemon juice
2 bunches fresh parsley,
   finely chopped
8 scallions, finely chopped

I bunch fresh mint, finely chopped
2 lbs ripe tomatoes, peeled,
   deseeded and chopped
salt and freshly ground pepper

I Put the bulgur wheat in a large bowl, cover with boiling water and let it soak for 30 minutes. Squeeze the grain with your hands to drain the water off and place it in a clean bowl.

2 Stir in all the remaining ingredients, and mix well. Let it stand for at least 1 hour before serving.

Bulgur Pilaf with Vegetables

. . . . **Ⓥ** . . . .

Makes 3 cups

Bulgur is cracked wheat that can be "cooked" by soaking in boiling liquid (see Tabouli, page 65), or by the absorption method, like rice. It can be served as a main dish, but it also goes well with anything that rice goes with. If you eat a lot of rice, bulgur makes a nice occasional change.

1 large mild onion,
   coarsely chopped
2-3 garlic cloves, crushed
1 carrot, coarsely chopped
2 cups vegetable stock
1 red pepper, peeled, deseeded
   and chopped
1 small zucchini, coarsely chopped

1 bunch fresh chives, snipped
3 tablespoons chopped fresh parsley
2 tablespoons shredded fresh mint
salt and freshly ground pepper
1 cup bulgur wheat

1 Put the onion, garlic, carrot and 1 cup of the stock in a heavy frying pan that can be covered. Cover, bring to a boil, and boil for 5-7 minutes. Uncover, reduce the heat slightly, and simmer briskly until the onion is tender and the liquid almost gone. Add the red pepper and zucchini, and a splash more stock, and cook for a few minutes more.

2 Stir the herbs into the vegetables and season with salt and pepper. Add the bulgur, and stir so everything is well combined. Pour in the remaining stock (which you have brought to a boil), and stir well.

3 Cover the pan and simmer over the lowest possible heat for about 20 minutes or until the bulgur is tender but not mushy, and all the liquid is absorbed. Fluff with a fork, taste and adjust the seasonings, then remove from the heat. Remove the lid, drape a tea-towel over the open pan, and replace the lid on the pan, over the tea-towel. Let stand for 10-15 minutes.

Orange-Scented Bulgur

· · · · · · · · · · · · · · **ⓥ** · · · · · · · · · · · · · ·

Makes 3 cups

This is my favorite bulgur recipe. My assistant and I once cooked it for 250 people—when the banquet was over there wasn't a single grain left.

1 mild onion, coarsely chopped
1 cup vegetable stock
1/2 teaspoon ground coriander
1/2 teaspoon ground cumin
2 garlic cloves, chopped
1/2 large orange

3/4 cup bulgur wheat
1 cup orange juice, strained
salt and freshly ground pepper
1-2 tablespoons chopped fresh
　cilantro (optional)

1 Put the onion, 1/2 cup of the stock, the spices and garlic in a frying pan that can be covered. Bring to a boil, then reduce the heat and simmer until the liquid has greatly reduced and the onions are "frying" in their own juices. Grate the peel from the orange right over the onions, so that some of the orange oils are added along with the peel. Add the bulgur, and stir until everything is well combined. Bring the remaining stock to a boil with the orange juice, and stir it into the bulgur. Season with salt and pepper.

2 Cover the pan and simmer over the lowest heat for about 20 minutes or until the bulgur is tender but not mushy, and all the liquid is absorbed. Fluff with a fork and remove from the heat. Drape a clean tea-towel over the open pan, and replace the lid over the towel. Let it stand for 5-10 minutes. Sprinkle the cilantro over the bulgur before serving.

Spicy Bulgur, Bean and Vegetable Casserole

. . . .

Makes 7 cups

For hearty appetites, this is a chili-like vegetable stew cooked with a generous measure of cracked wheat. Serve in big soup bowls, and let everyone top their portion with their own selection of garnishes.

1/2 cup bulgur wheat
2 cups boiling vegetable stock
1 large mild onion,
   coarsely chopped
3 celery stalks, cut into
   1/2-inch slices
3 carrots, coarsely chopped
3 peppers, peeled, deseeded and
   coarsely chopped (1 red, 1 yellow
   and 1 green if available)
4 garlic cloves, crushed
1 tablespoon mild chili powder
   (or to taste)
1/2 teaspoon ground coriander
2 teaspoons ground cumin

1/2 teaspoon paprika
2 14-oz cans of
   chopped tomatoes
1 15-oz can of red kidney beans,
   drained and rinsed
1 15-oz can of chickpeas,
   drained and rinsed
1 large cauliflower, separated
   into florets
salt and freshly ground pepper

TO GARNISH
cottage cheese
grated Parmesan cheese
chopped fresh cilantro

1 Combine the bulgur with 1 cup of the hot stock in a bowl, cover and set aside.

2 Put the vegetables, 1 cup of the remaining stock, and the spices in a flameproof casserole. Bring to a boil, then reduce the heat and simmer briskly, stirring, until the vegetables and spices are "frying" in their own juices, and the vegetables are tender.

3 Stir in the tomatoes, bulgur, kidney beans, chickpeas and cauliflower, and season with salt and pepper. Simmer, partially covered, for 30 minutes or until the mixture is thick and the cauliflower tender but not mushy. Arrange garnishes in bowls and serve with the casserole.

Ⓥ Omit the cottage cheese garnish.

Couscous

Couscous is made up of tiny bits of semolina: you might say that it is a collection of tiny grains of pasta. Because most packaged couscous that you find in supermarkets and health food stores is precooked, it needs only a brief soaking in hot liquid. Couscous is an excellent accompaniment to any vegetable stew.

Basic Couscous

. . . . **V** . . . .

Makes 4 cups

1 1/2 cups couscous
2 cups well-seasoned boiling stock

1 Combine the couscous and boiling liquid in a large bowl, and let it soak for 10-15 minutes or until the liquid is absorbed and the grains tender. Fluff with a fork.

Couscous with Vegetable Curry

V · **Z**

Makes 6 cups

2 1/2 cups vegetable stock
1 large mild onion, coarsely chopped
2-3 garlic cloves, crushed
1 1/2 teaspoons ground cumin
1 1/2 teaspoons ground coriander
1/4 teaspoon ground allspice
1/4 teaspoon cayenne
1/2 teaspoon ground ginger
1 teaspoon ground turmeric
1 teaspoon paprika
3 celery stalks, cut into
    1/2-inch slices
3 carrots, coarsely chopped
3 small white turnips, coarsely
    chopped

3 peppers (1 red, 1 green, 1 yellow),
    peeled, deseeded and
    coarsely chopped
1 fennel bulb, cut into 1/2-inch slices
1 15-oz can of chickpeas, drained
    and rinsed
6 tablespoons lemon juice
salt and freshly ground pepper
one quantity Basic Couscous
    (see page 69)
4 tablespoons chopped fresh parsley
2 tablespoons chopped
    fresh cilantro

1 Put 1 cup of the stock, onion, garlic and spices in a frying pan. Cover, bring to a boil, and boil for 5 minutes. Stir in the celery, carrots, turnips, peppers, fennel and another 1/4 cup of the stock. Simmer, stirring frequently, until the vegetables and spices are "frying" in their own juices.

2 Stir in the remaining ingredients (except the herbs and couscous), including the remaining 1 1/4 cups of stock. Season to taste with salt and pepper, then cover and simmer gently for 15 minutes.

3 Arrange the cooked couscous in a mound on a large platter, and surround with the vegetables. Sprinkle with the herbs.

Couscous Salad

· · · · · · · · · · · · **Ⓥ** · · · · · · · · · · · ·

Makes 5 cups

This is one of my stand-bys for low-fat luncheon buffets. It is very easy to make, looks beautiful on the table, and seems to please most people, even those who have never had couscous before.

1 cup boiling, well-seasoned stock
6 oz couscous
1 15-oz can of chickpeas,
  drained and rinsed
1 red pepper, peeled, deseeded
  and diced
3-4 scallions, sliced thinly
1 small zucchini, diced
1 small carrot, diced
3-4 tablespoons chopped
  fresh parsley

3-4 tablespoons shredded
  fresh mint
freshly ground pepper

DRESSING
1 cup vegetable stock
1 1/2–2 1/2 tablespoons
  balsamic vinegar
1-2 limes
2 garlic cloves, crushed
1/2 teaspoon ground cumin
1-2 pinches of cayenne

1 To make the dressing, put half the stock in a small frying pan, and add 1/2 tablespoon balsamic vinegar, the juice of 1/2 lime, the garlic, cumin and cayenne. Cover, bring to a boil, and boil for 5 minutes. Uncover, reduce the heat slightly, and simmer briskly until the garlic is very tender, and the liquid has cooked down to a syrupy glaze.

2 Add the remaining stock and boil until reduced by about half. Stir in a further 1 tablespoon balsamic vinegar and the juice of 1/2 lime. Keep warm.

3 For the salad, mix the boiling stock and couscous together in a large bowl. Cover with plastic wrap and let it stand for 10 minutes. Uncover, and fluff up with a fork.

4 Toss in all the remaining ingredients, except the dressing, and season with pepper.

5 Pour the warm dressing over the couscous and toss with two spoons. Taste and add more seasonings, vinegar and lime juice, if necessary.

Couscous Salad with Smoked Tofu and Oranges

Makes 4 cups

Oranges, smoked tofu, and fresh and spicy citrus dressing enhance the tender, wheaty couscous grains.

COUSCOUS
juice and finely grated peel of
    half a lime and half an orange
1 1/2 cups vegetable stock
3/4 cup couscous
salt and freshly ground pepper

DRESSING
2 tablespoons balsamic vinegar
2 tablespoons lime juice
2 tablespoons orange juice
1 teaspoon soy sauce
several dashes tabasco sauce
several dashes teriyaki sauce
1 garlic clove, crushed (optional)

SALAD
1 large seedless orange, peeled
    of all skin and pith, and diced
1/2 lb smoked tofu, cut into
    1/2-inch cubes
2 tablespoons chopped fresh parsley
4 scallions, sliced
2 tablespoons shredded fresh mint

GARNISH
halved cherry tomatoes
small wedges of lemon, lime
    and orange

1 For the couscous, mix the lime juice, orange juice and grated peel in a measuring cup and add enough stock to bring the mixture to 1 cup. Pour into a saucepan and bring to a boil.

2 Pour this hot mixture over the couscous in a large bowl, season with salt and pepper to taste, and mix well. Let the mixture steep for 10-15 minutes or until the liquid is absorbed and the couscous grains are tender. Fluff up with a fork. Whisk together all the dressing ingredients.

3 Put all the salad ingredients together in a bowl. Add half the dressing. Toss together well, then add to the couscous with the remaining dressing. Toss gently to mix, then pile onto a platter and surround with the garnishes.

Roasted Buckwheat Groats (Kasha)

Kasha, an ancient and sustaining grain-like food, is not a grain at all, but a botanical fruit—the split, roasted seed of buckwheat, a flowery, distant relative of rhubarb. Kasha originated on the border between Manchuria and Russia, and has been a staple of Russian cooking for centuries. Kasha is not exactly an aristocratic food: it has an earthy, peasant quality that will sustain people through winters of the soul, as well as climatic winters.

Being of Russian-Jewish ancestry, I grew up with kasha, and I still regard a warming bowlful, garnished with brown onions and sautéed mushrooms, the epitome of soul food. Plain kasha is a perfect foil for saucy vegetable stews; with the mushroom and onion garnish and a side dish of yogurt or cottage cheese and chopped herbs, it keeps the wolf from the door with a vengeance. Seek out roasted buckwheat groats in health food stores; if you haven't tried it before, you are in for a treat.

Basic Kasha

· ·

Makes 3 cups

2 egg whites, lightly beaten
6 oz kasha (roasted
  buckwheat groats)

2 cups boiling vegetable stock
salt and freshly ground pepper

1 Heat a large, heavy-bottomed saucepan.

2 Stir the egg white into the kasha, mixing until the grains are well coated. Tip it into the hot pan.

3 With a wooden spoon or spatula, stir the kasha over moderate heat for about 5 minutes or until each grain is dry and separate, and the kasha smells deliciously toasty.

4 Stir the boiling stock into the kasha, season, cover and simmer over the lowest heat for 30 minutes. Remove from the heat, uncover, and drape a clean tea-towel over the open pan. Replace the lid over the tea-towel, and let it stand for 5-10 minutes or until the liquid is absorbed and the kasha is fluffy and tender, each grain separate.

Kasha with Mushrooms and Browned Onions

Makes 4 cups

This is a classic, but I have eliminated all traces of chicken fat, and then reconstructed it with the non-fat mushroom sauté method using sherry, teriyaki and stock. The result is a much lighter, fresher, but still deeply satisfying version of the original.

1/2 oz dried mushrooms (look for *cèpes* or the Italian counterpart, *porcini*)
2 egg whites, lightly beaten
3/4 cup kasha (roasted buckwheat groats)
2 cups vegetable stock

1/2 lb fresh mushrooms, coarsely chopped
1/4 cup dry sherry
generous dash of soy or teriyaki sauce
I mild onion, coarsely chopped
salt and freshly ground pepper

1 Rinse the dried mushrooms well under cold running water. Put them in a bowl, cover generously with hot water, and leave to soak for 20 minutes. Tip the mushrooms into a sieve lined with a double layer of coffee filter papers or muslin to strain off the soaking water. Reserve mushrooms and water. Briefly rinse the soaked mushrooms once more under cold running water. Trim off and discard any tough stems, then coarsely chop the mushrooms.

2 Stir the egg whites into the kasha, mixing until the grains are well coated with the egg. Heat a large, heavy-bottomed saucepan, tip in the kasha and stir with a wooden spoon or spatula over moderate heat for about 5 minutes or until each grain is dry and separate, and the kasha smells deliciously toasty. Remove from the heat.

3 Combine 1 cup of the stock with 1 cup of the reserved mushroom soaking liquid, pour into a saucepan and bring to a boil. Stir the boiling liquid into the kasha, cover the pan and simmer over the lowest heat for 30 minutes. Remove from the heat, uncover, and drape a clean tea-towel over the open pan. Replace the lid over the tea-towel and let it stand for 5-10 minutes or until the liquid is absorbed and the kasha is fluffy and tender, with each grain separate.

4 Meanwhile, put the soaked mushrooms in a heavy-bottomed frying pan with the fresh mushrooms, 2 fl oz of the remaining stock, the sherry and the soy or teriyaki sauce. Bring to a boil, then reduce the heat and simmer briskly, stirring occasionally, until the liquid is almost gone, and the mushrooms are "frying" in their own juices. Transfer to a bowl and set aside. Wipe out the frying pan.

5 Put the onion in the frying pan with the remaining stock, cover and bring to a boil. Reduce the heat slightly and simmer briskly for 5-7 minutes. Uncover and continue cooking until the onion is meltingly tender and syrupy. Add to the mushrooms. Taste, and season with salt and pepper if necessary.

6 When the kasha is ready, combine it with the onion and the mushrooms.

NOTE

This may be prepared in advance and reheated in the microwave or conventional oven. To make the classic and beloved Russian-Jewish dish, *Kasha Varnishkas*, mix equal amounts of this kasha with freshly boiled and drained bow-tie-shaped pasta.

Millet

Millet is perhaps better known as bird food, but birds eat the unhulled variety. The hull is inedible for humans, presumably because we lack gizzards. Hulled millet, available in health food stores, has a delicate nut-like flavor and a pleasing chewy texture. Toasting it first in a heavy-bottomed pan brings out the delicate flavor.

Chinese-Style Millet and Mushrooms in Lettuce Parcels

· · · · · · · · · · · · · · **(V)** · · · · · · · · · · · · ·

Makes 4 cups millet and mushrooms mixture

1 oz dried shiitake mushrooms
  (about 10)
1 head of lettuce, such as iceberg
1 cup millet
2 garlic cloves, crushed
1/2-inch piece of fresh ginger,
  peeled and crushed
7 scallions, sliced
10 fresh mushrooms, cut into
  quarters or eighths
1/4 cup dry sherry

several dashes of teriyaki sauce
1 1/2 cups vegetable stock
salt and freshly ground pepper
juice of 1 lime
juice of 1/2 large orange
2 teaspoons sugar
8-oz can of water chestnuts,
  drained and quartered
chopped fresh cilantro, to taste
sliced scallions, to serve

1 Rinse the dried mushrooms under cold running water. Put them in a bowl, cover with plenty of hot water (about 2 cups), and let soak for 20 minutes.

2 Separate the leaves from the lettuce, wash well and shake dry. Trim off and discard the tough stem from each leaf. Wrap the leaves in a tea-towel and refrigerate until serving time.

3 Put the millet in a heavy-bottomed frying pan and heat gently, stirring constantly for about 3 minutes or until the grains smell beautifully toasty (not scorched) and some of them begin to pop. Tip the millet into a bowl.

4 Tip the dried mushrooms and their soaking liquid into a sieve lined with a double layer of muslin or coffee filter papers set over a bowl. Strain off the liquid. Reserve the mushrooms and the liquid. Cut the mushrooms into 1/2-inch pieces, discarding any tough stems.

5 Put *half* the soaked mushrooms in a heavy-bottomed saucepan or flameproof casserole with the garlic, ginger, scallions, fresh mushrooms, sherry, teriyaki sauce and 2-3 fl oz of the reserved mushroom soaking liquid. Bring to a boil, then reduce the heat and simmer, stirring occasionally, until the mushrooms are tender and most of the liquid has been absorbed.

6 Mix the stock with 1 cup of the remaining mushroom liquid, and add to the mushroom mixture with the millet. Season with salt and pepper. Bring to a boil, cover and simmer on the lowest heat for 20 minutes. Remove from the heat, uncover, and fluff up with a fork. Drape a clean tea-towel over the open pan. Replace the lid over the tea-towel and leave to stand for 5-10 minutes.

7 Mix the lime and orange juice with 1/2 cup of the remaining mushroom soaking liquid, and stir in the sugar. When the millet is ready, spoon it into a bowl. Add the lime and orange mixture, the water chestnuts, remaining soaked mushrooms, and some chopped cilantro. Toss with two spoons to combine thoroughly.

8 To serve, mound the millet in the center of a large platter. Sprinkle with scallions and additional cilantro, and surround with the lettuce leaves. To eat, spoon some of the grain onto a lettuce leaf, roll it up and eat with your fingers. Forget knives and forks for this one.

Polenta

Polenta is a kind of savory porridge made from corn meal. It is a staple of Alpine Italy and the Swiss Ticino. It is also a staple in parts of Africa, where it is known as "mealy-mealy"; in Rumania, where it is called "mamaliga"; and in the southern U.S., where it bears the unlovely name "corn meal mush." Corn originated in the New World; it didn't reach Italy until the seventeenth century, but despite its relative youth in that part of the world, it has become a deeply entrenched staple. If you can't find quick-cooking polenta, use the ordinary kind, but cook it for 10-15 minutes longer in step 1.

Polenta and Eggplant Gratin

. . . .

Serves 6

2 14-oz cans of chopped
   tomatoes
4 cups vegetable stock
6 oz quick-cooking polenta
salt and freshly ground pepper
1 large onion, coarsely chopped
1 red or yellow pepper, peeled,
   deseeded and coarsely chopped
2 garlic cloves, crushed

1/2 teaspoon dried basil
1/2 cup dry red wine
4-6 ripe tomatoes, peeled,
   deseeded and chopped
2-3 tablespoons tomato purée
4 tablespoons chopped fresh parsley
2 medium eggplants, cut into
   1/2-inch slices and grilled
   (see page 129)
6 tablespoons grated
   Parmesan cheese

1 Tip the canned tomatoes into a bowl, reserving the empty cans. Wash out the cans thoroughly and leave upside-down to drain.

2 Put the 3 1/2 cups stock in a large saucepan, and bring to a boil. With a wire whisk, whisk in the polenta, whisking well so the mixture does not form lumps. Bring back to a boil, then immediately lower the heat and cook over low heat, stirring with a wooden spoon for about 5 minutes or until the polenta is smooth and very thick. As it cooks, taste, and season with salt if needed. Be careful the mixture does not scorch. Pack into the two cleaned tomato cans, cool, cover with plastic wrap and refrigerate. Preheat the oven to 350°F.

3 Put the onion, red or yellow pepper, garlic, basil, wine and 1/2 cup stock in a saucepan, cover and bring to a boil. Reduce the heat and simmer for about 10 minutes. Uncover and continue cooking until the vegetables are tender and the liquid almost gone. Stir in the canned and fresh tomatoes and simmer for 15-20 minutes. Stir in the tomato purée and parsley, and simmer for 5 minutes more. Season with salt and pepper, remove from the heat and set aside.

4 Push or shake the polenta out of the cans (it will come out in compact cylinders). The top of each cylinder will be crusty; cut a thin slice off the top and discard. Cut the remainder into roughly 1/2-inch slices and arrange in a shallow baking dish, alternating each slice with a slice of grilled eggplant. Spread the sauce over them and sprinkle with Parmesan. Bake for 30 minutes or until hot and bubbly.

VARIATION

Grilled Polenta with Fava Bean-Corn Stew

polenta, cooked and packed into cans (see step 2, above)
Fava Bean-Corn Stew (see page 107)

thinly sliced low-fat mozzarella cheese
freshly ground pepper

1 Preheat the grill to its highest heat.

2 Shake the polenta "cylinders" out of the cans. Cut a thin slice from the top of each and discard. Slice the polenta and arrange in one layer on a non-stick baking sheet. Grill, 6 inches from the heat, for 4-6 minutes or until beginning to brown on top.

3 Spoon a generous quantity of the stew onto each polenta round, and top with a slice of mozzarella. Sprinkle generously with freshly ground pepper. Grill 3 inches from the heat for 3-5 minutes or until the cheese is melted, bubbly and speckled with brown. Lift the slices off the sheet with a spatula, and place on plates. Alternatively, the polenta rounds can be placed in a baking dish in one layer, covered with stew, and cheese slices laid on top. Grill until bubbly and lightly browned.

Savory Polenta Pie with Garlic and Scallions

. . . .

Makes 8-inch pie

Try polenta cooked with scallions, flavored with cheese, molded into a cake tin, and baked until the wafting fragrance drives you mad with hunger. A wedge of this is great with a steaming bowl of soup, or with some of the bean dishes or vegetable stews in other chapters of this book. This pie serves 6 people.

12 scallions, thinly sliced
1-2 garlic cloves, finely chopped
6 cups vegetable stock
12 1/2 oz quick-cooking polenta

salt and freshly ground pepper
6 tablespoons grated Parmesan
   cheese

1 Preheat the oven to 350°F.

2 Put the scallions, garlic and 1 cup of the stock in a heavy-bottomed saucepan. Cover, bring to a boil and boil for 5 minutes, then uncover, reduce the heat slightly, and simmer briskly until the onions and garlic are tender, and the liquid is almost gone.

3 Pour in the remaining stock, and bring almost to a boil. When just below boiling point, pour in the polenta in a steady stream, stirring constantly with a wire whisk. Switch from the whisk to a wooden spoon, and cook, stirring, for about 5 minutes or until the mixture is thick and smooth. (Watch out for volcanic bubbles; wear an oven glove to protect your hand and arm.) Season with salt and pepper, and stir in the Parmesan cheese.

4 Spoon and scrape the mixture into a non-stick, 8-inch-diameter round cake tin with a removable bottom. Smooth the surface with the back of the spoon. Bake in the oven for 25-30 minutes or until firm and fragrant. Cool on a wire rack for 5 minutes, then loosen all around the edges and remove the sides of the tin. Cut into wedges.

Pasta

Lemony Pasta Pilaf

· · · · · · · · · · · · **V** · · · · · · · · · · · ·

Very small pasta shapes can be cooked like rice by the absorption method. A good stock is imperative (see page 8 for a discussion of vegetable stocks). I make this frequently, because it's perfect after a long tiring day, when something simple, unchallenging, easy to prepare and to eat, and—most important—deeply comforting, is needed. I usually make it with tiny pasta shells, but any small pasta will do. Once, in desperation (I had run out of pasta shells), I made this with tiny dinosaur-shaped pasta I found lurking in the back of the cupboard, left over from a godson's visit. I enjoyed every swallow, although I did feel a little foolish shoveling in shoals of tyrannosaurs and brontosaurs! Serve this plain, or with a small shower of grated medium-fat cheese stirred in, or with a dollop of tomato or pepper sauce (see pages 92 and 99) ladled on top. If you want to wake up your palate, rather than lull it into gentle calm, top the hot pasta pilaf with icy Mexican Salsa (see page 187). See the note on page 50 regarding serving quantities.

2 cups vegetable stock	juice of 1/2-1 small lemon
8 oz mini-pasta shells	salt and freshly ground pepper

1 Put the stock in a heavy-bottomed saucepan that can be tightly covered, and bring to a boil. Stir in the pasta and the juice of 1/2 a lemon. Season with pepper and a little salt, if necessary, and bring back to a boil. Stir once, turn the heat to low, cover the pan and simmer for 5-8 minutes or until most of the liquid has been absorbed (exact timing depends on the pan, the pasta, and your stove).

2 Uncover the pan, stir in the juice of the second lemon half (if you wish), and remove from the heat. Drape a clean tea-towel over the open pan, replace the lid over the towel, and let stand for 5 minutes or until the pasta is quite tender and the liquid absorbed. It will have an almost buttery quality—consider it gastronomic emotional therapy!

Pasta with Fresh Vegetable Sauce

· · · · · · · · · · · · **Ⓥ** · · · · · · · · · · · ·

Serves 2–4

Put the water for the pasta in a large saucepan and prepare this fresh and delicate sauce while it comes to a boil. I use penne for this.

6 oz button mushrooms, quartered	I fennel bulb
I bunch of scallions, thinly sliced	I medium zucchini
I garlic clove, crushed	4 fresh, ripe, flavorful tomatoes
I cup vegetable stock	4-5 fresh basil leaves, shredded
I red and I yellow pepper, cut lengthwise into their natural sections and deseeded	salt and freshly ground pepper
	12 oz–I lb pasta

I Fill a large saucepan with water for the pasta, and bring it to a boil.

2 Meanwhile, put the mushrooms, scallions, garlic and about 1/2 cup of the stock in a flameproof casserole. Bring to a boil, then reduce the heat and simmer until the vegetables are tender, and most of the liquid has cooked away.

3 Meanwhile, peel the pepper pieces with a swivel-bladed peeler, and cut them into 1-inch squares. Trim the fennel and cut in half lengthwise and then slice. Cut the zucchini into 1/2-inch slices.

4 Add the peppers to the mushroom mixture with the remaining stock, and cook, stirring occasionally, until the peppers are almost tender. Add the fennel and zucchini, and cook, stirring, for a few minutes more or until all the vegetables are tender.

5 Meanwhile, put the tomatoes in a sieve and dip them into the boiling pasta water for 10 seconds. Refresh briefly under cold running water, then peel, deseed and roughly dice. Add to the vegetables with the shredded basil, and season. Cook gently until the tomatoes have lost their shape, and the mixture is thick and savory.

6 Cook the pasta in the boiling water until *al dente,* drain it well, then toss it with the sauce directly in the casserole. Serve at once.

Pasta with Creamy Cauliflower Sauce

. . . .

Serves 2–4

Pasta tossed with a good tomato and cauliflower sauce and creamy ricotta cheese makes a hearty meal. For a non-dairy version, prepare to the end of step 1, and toss the vegetable sauce with the hot pasta. In fact, the cauliflower in tomato sauce is perfectly delicious all by itself as well, without the pasta.

4-5 scallions, sliced
2-3 dry-packed sun-dried
   tomatoes, chopped
   (use scissors)
2 black olives in brine, drained
   and flesh slivered off the stones
1-2 garlic cloves, crushed
1 cup vegetable stock
14-oz can of chopped tomatoes
2 cups tomato purée

salt and freshly ground pepper
1 cauliflower, separated into
   florets and steamed
1 lb pasta shapes
7 oz ricotta cheese, at room
   temperature
3 tablespoons grated Parmesan
   cheese
2 tablespoons shredded fresh basil

1 Put the onions, sun-dried tomatoes, olive slivers, garlic and stock in a large heavy-bottomed saucepan. Bring to a boil, then reduce the heat and simmer until the onions and garlic are tender and the stock almost gone. Stir in the tomatoes and tomato purée, season with salt and pepper, and simmer for 10 minutes more. Stir in the cauliflower and simmer for another 5-10 minutes or until the cauliflower is very tender and imbued with the taste of the sauce.

2 Meanwhile, cook the pasta in boiling water until *al dente.*

3 Put the ricotta in a large bowl, and whisk in the Parmesan. Stir the basil into the cauliflower sauce, and fold into the ricotta mixture. Drain the pasta and toss with the sauce. Serve at once.

Grilled Vegetable Lasagna

Serves 4–6

A soufflé-like mixture of low-fat semi-soft cheese and beaten egg whites takes the place of the usual high-fat white sauce in this splendid lasagna. The baking time given results in a creamy-textured layer. Cook it longer and the cheese-egg layer will set—not a bad thing, but I prefer the creamy texture.

I like to use fresh lasagna sheets for this recipe. They are available from Italian delicatessens and speciality shops, and sometimes from the refrigerator sections of supermarkets. If you can't find fresh pasta, or if you are in a hurry, use dried lasagna. There is no need to cook dried lasagna first: just layer it with the other ingredients, and bake. You may need more tomato sauce when you use dried lasagna.

six 5 x 6-inch sheets of fresh lasagna
1 small eggplant, sliced and grilled
  (see page 124)
2 small zucchini, sliced and
  grilled (see page 130)
2 red or yellow peppers,
  grilled (see page 131)
2 cups tomato sauce
  (see pages 91-92)

1 lb low-fat semi-soft cheese
8 oz half-fat mozzarella cheese,
  shredded
salt and freshly ground pepper
3 egg whites, beaten to firm peaks
4-5 tablespoons grated
  Parmesan cheese

1 Preheat the oven to 400°F.

2 Cook the fresh lasagna sheets according to package instructions, but undercook them slightly. Drain them, spread them out on a clean tea-towel, and blot them dry with paper towels.

3 Chop up the grilled vegetables with kitchen scissors, and stir them into the tomato sauce.

4 Put the low-fat cheese and mozzarella cheese in a food processor. Season with salt and pepper, and process until well amalgamated. Transfer to a bowl and stir in a quarter of the beaten egg whites. Fold in the remainder.

5 Spread a thin layer of tomato sauce in the bottom of a 12 x 7-inch baking dish, and cover with a layer of three sheets of lasagna. Spread on the cheese mixture and sprinkle with 2 tablespoons Parmesan. Cover with three more sheets of lasagna, spread on the remaining tomato sauce and sprinkle on the remaining cheese.

6 Cover and bake in the oven for 15 minutes. Uncover and bake for a further 15-20 minutes or until puffy and bubbling.

Macaroni with Creamy Cheese Sauce

· ·

Serves 4–6

Macaroni and cheese doesn't get any easier than this—hot pasta tossed with low-fat cheese and grated hard cheese in a warm bowl. As you mix the pasta into the cheese mixture, it forms a sauce that oozes into the cavities of the pasta in a seductive manner.

I lb pasta shells,
   elbow macaroni or penne
2 cups of low-fat semi-soft cheese
   at room temperature

4 tablespoons grated Parmesan
   cheese or other medium-fat
   hard cheese
1/2 cup skim milk,
   at room temperature
freshly ground pepper (optional)

I Cook the pasta in boiling water until *al dente*.

2 Meanwhile, process the two cheeses, and skim milk in a food processor until very well combined. Scrape into a warm bowl.

3 Drain the pasta, and immediately toss it into the cheese mixture. Grind in some pepper, if desired, and serve at once.

Bread Puddings

Savory bread puddings make satisfying, filling and nutritious family meals. They are not desperate measures for using up old bread, but well thought-out and constructed dishes that have plenty of merit of their own (although they do—when all is said and done—use up old bread in a most efficient way).

   The ingredients can be combined hours ahead of time and then left in the fridge to soak. The more efficiently the custard soaks into the bread cubes, the better the texture, and the better the rising power of the pudding. To serve for brunch, mix the ingredients the night before; for supper, mix them in the morning. If you plan to bake the pudding immediately, be sure to mix the ingredients very well, so maximum soaking occurs.

Bread and Corn Pudding

· ·

Serves 2–4

5 scallions, sliced
I fresh chile pepper, deseeded
   and finely chopped
1/2 teaspoon ground cumin
1/2 cup vegetable stock
1/2 cup skim milk
2 tablespoons skim-milk
   powder
14-oz can of creamed corn
I egg

3 egg whites
6 oz stale bread, cut into
   1/2-inch cubes
about 12 oz canned
   corn kernels, drained
4 oz low-fat mozzarella cheese,
   cubed
salt and freshly ground pepper
1-2 tablespoons grated Parmesan,
   half-fat cheddar or Swiss cheese

I Preheat the oven to 350°F.

2 Put the scallions, chile and cumin in a heavy-bottomed saucepan with the stock. Bring to a boil, then reduce the heat and simmer until the onions are tender and the stock almost gone.

3 Mix the milk and skim-milk powder, and put in a large bowl with the creamed corn, the whole egg and the egg whites. Beat well together, then stir in the bread, corn kernels, mozzarella, and the onion mixture. Season with salt and pepper, and use two spoons to toss everything together very well, so that the bread absorbs the liquid.

4 Spoon the mixture into a 10-inch-diameter round ovenproof dish that is about 2 inches deep (or use a square casserole). Bake in the oven for about 40 minutes, sprinkling on the cheese 5-10 minutes before the pie is cooked. When it is puffy, browned, and a knife inserted near the center comes out clean, remove from the oven and serve, cut into wedges.

Bread and Caramelized Onion Pudding

Serves 4–6

Like French onion soup without the soup, this main-dish bread pudding combines melted cheese with shreds of caramelized onion and savory custard-soaked cubes of bread. It rises almost like a soufflé.

1 large garlic clove, halved
4 large mild onions
1 1/2 cups vegetable stock
1/4 cup dry vermouth
1/2 lb stale crusty French bread,
   cut into 1/2-inch cubes
2 eggs

2 egg whites
2 cups skim milk
3 tablespoons skim-milk
   powder
4 tablespoons grated Parmesan or
   low-fat Swiss cheese
salt and freshly ground pepper

1 Preheat the oven to 350°F.

2 Choose a shallow round or oval dish and rub it thoroughly with the cut side of the garlic clove. Discard the garlic.

3 Cut the onions in half and slice into thin halfmoons. Put the onions in a deep 10-inch heavy-bottomed frying pan and add the stock. Cover and boil for about 10 minutes.

4 Uncover the pan, reduce the heat, and simmer, stirring occasionally, until the onions are meltingly tender, beginning to turn amber, and the liquid is almost gone. Pour in the vermouth and simmer briskly until the liquid cooks away, stirring and scraping up any browned bits from the bottom of the pan.

5 Toss the bread and onions together in a large bowl.

6 Beat the eggs and egg whites lightly together. Mix the milk and skim-milk powder together, and beat into the egg mixture. Season with salt and pepper. Pour the mixture evenly over the bread and sprinkle on the grated cheese. Gently toss and mix with two spoons to saturate the bread with the egg mixture. Pour the mixture into the dish.

7 Bake in the oven for 45-50 minutes or until set, puffed and golden. (A knife inserted near the center should emerge clean.)

Sauces

A repertoire of basic sauces can help glamorize a bowl of pasta, a boiled potato, a bowl of mashed potatoes or steamed vegetables. But a sauce should be more than decoration or fancy dressing—it should add its own good measure of nutrition as well. All of these sauces are based on vegetables, instead of on flour-fat roux, butter-egg yolk emulsions, or full-fat dairy products. And all of them (except the Colombian Tomato-Cheese Sauce) are suitable for vegans.

Classic Slim Cuisine Tomato Sauce

. . . . **Ⓥ** . . **Ⓩ** . . . .

Makes 3 cups

Tomato sauce is one of the most useful of sauces, and one of the easiest as well, given the wide variety of excellent canned and bottled tomato products available in every supermarket. My basic tomato sauce, a staple in my Slim Cuisine series of books as well as in my personal cookery, is worth making in quantity and then freezing in small portions. If you plan to freeze it, omit the fresh herbs. Add them after thawing and reheating. Dried herbs can be added before freezing. The sauce is superb on pasta or pizza, or as part of countless recipes. I have one reader who spreads it on hot toast!

3 shallots finely chopped or
  I mild onion, chopped
2 garlic cloves, crushed
pinch of cayenne
3/4 cup vegetable stock
3/4 cup dry red wine,
  white wine or vermouth
I tablespoon chopped fresh basil
  or I/4 teaspoon dried basil
I tablespoon chopped fresh thyme
  or I/4 teaspoon dried

I tablespoon chopped fresh
  oregano or I/4 teaspoon dried
  oregano
3 I4-oz cans of
  chopped tomatoes
salt and freshly ground pepper
2 tablespoons tomato purée
I tablespoon chopped fresh
  parsley

I Put the shallots or onion, garlic, cayenne, stock, wine and dried herbs, if using, in a heavy-bottomed frying pan. Cover and boil for 5-7 minutes. Uncover, reduce the heat and simmer briskly until the liquid is almost gone.

2 Stir in the tomatoes, and season with salt and pepper. Simmer, partially covered, for 20 minutes. Stir in the tomato purée and simmer for 10 minutes more. If you are using fresh herbs, stir them in now, including the parsley. Taste and adjust the seasonings.

Quick Tomato Sauce

· · · · · · · · · · · **V** · · **Z** · · · · · · · · · · · · ·

Makes 3 cups

A can of tomato purée, tomatoes, and a garlic-olive infusion produce a spectacular tomato sauce in less than 20 minutes.

5-6 scallions, sliced
3 black olives in brine, drained
   and flesh slivered off the stones
3-4 dry-packed, sun-dried
   tomatoes, chopped
   (use scissors)
1-2 garlic cloves, crushed
1-2 pinches crushed dried chilies

1-2 pinches dried oregano
8 cups vegetable stock
2 cups tomato purée
1 14-oz can of chopped tomatoes
freshly ground pepper

1 Put the onions, olive pieces, sun-dried tomatoes, garlic, chile, oregano and stock in a heavy-bottomed frying pan. Cover and boil for 3-4 minutes. Uncover, reduce the heat, and simmer until the onions and garlic are tender and the liquid has cooked down considerably and become syrupy.

2 Stir in the tomato purée and chopped tomatoes, and grind in some pepper. Simmer briskly for 10-15 minutes or until thick and savory. Taste and adjust the seasoning, if necessary, before serving.

Roasted Tomato Ketchup

· · · · · · · · · · · **Ⓥ** · · **Ⓩ** · · · · · · · · · ·

Makes 1 1/2 cups

For oven-fried potatoes (see page 175), an accompanying puddle of tomato sauce for dabbling is a nice touch. Eating fried potatoes with your fingers, dunking the pieces into the sauce between bites, is like being a child again. When good tomatoes are available, char them in the oven (or you could put them on the barbecue), then peel them and use to make a thick, smoky purée.

15 very ripe, flavorful,
   juicy tomatoes, cored
2 large mild onions, finely chopped
4 garlic cloves, crushed

1/2 cup red wine
1/2 cup vegetable stock
salt and freshly ground pepper

1 Preheat the oven to 425°F.

2 Put the tomatoes in one layer on a baking sheet, and bake, uncovered, in the oven for about 30 minutes or until blistered and charred. Let cool slightly.

3 While the tomatoes are baking, put the onions, garlic, wine and stock in a heavy-bottomed frying pan. Cover, bring to a boil, and boil for 5-7 minutes. Uncover, reduce the heat and simmer briskly until the onions are tender and beginning to brown, and the liquid is almost gone.

4 When the tomatoes have cooled somewhat, squeeze them out of their skins into the frying pan. Discard the skins. Simmer the tomato pulp for about 20 minutes or until it is thick. Season with salt and pepper, and leave to cool slightly.

5 Pour the sauce into a blender and purée until smooth. Rub through a sieve to eliminate the seeds.

Gravy

Makes 4 cups

Puréed cooked vegetables can be used to make a rich-tasting sauce, although the fat level is virtually nil. The red wine adds luxurious depth to the sauce, but it is simmered briskly so that the alcohol evaporates, leaving flavor, but no inebriating quality. Freeze the sauce in small containers, so it is available when you need it. The best way to serve gravy? Scoop a generous serving of mashed potatoes (or mashed potatoes mixed with puréed Foil-Roasted Vegetables—see page 136—onto a plate. Make a deep dent in the mound, ladle out a generous measure of gravy, and overfill the dent so that the gravy overflows and dribbles down the sides of the mound. Surround with more gravy. Eat with a large spoon.

4 shallots or I small onion, chopped
I large mild onion, chopped
2 celery stalks, chopped
2 garlic cloves, crushed
2 carrots, chopped

6 cups vegetable stock
2 cups dry red wine
I 14-oz can of chopped tomatoes
salt and freshly ground pepper

1 Put the vegetables in a heavy-bottomed frying pan with 1 cup of the stock. Cover and boil for 5 minutes.

2 Uncover, reduce the heat slightly, and simmer, stirring occasionally, until the vegetables are tender and the liquid almost gone.

3 Stir in the wine, bay leaf and tomatoes. Simmer briskly, uncovered, for 15 minutes.

4 Stir in the remaining stock, and simmer for 15 minutes, stirring occasionally. Remove the bay leaf and let cool slightly.

5 Pour into a blender and purée until smooth. Sieve the gravy into a bowl, rubbing with a wooden spoon. Season with salt and pepper and reheat gently.

Spicy Bean Sauce

· · · · · · · · · · · **V** · · **Z** · · · · · · · · · · · ·

Makes 5 cups

Lavish this lively sauce over pasta, couscous, polenta or any of your favorite grains. It's good in a rice crust too (see page 56), with a little low-fat mozzarella melted on top.

l large mild onion, coarsely
   chopped
2 garlic cloves, crushed
2 celery stalks, cut into
   1/2-inch slices
l teaspoon dried thyme
l bay leaf
l teaspoon dried tarragon
l teaspoon ground cumin
pinch of cayenne
1/2 teaspoon ground allspice

3/4 cup vegetable stock
1/4 cup red wine
2 red peppers, peeled, deseeded
   and coarsely chopped
2 14-oz cans of chopped
   tomatoes
l tablespoon drained capers
l 15-oz can of red kidney, or
   pinto beans, drained and rinsed
salt and freshly ground pepper

l Put the onion, garlic, celery, herbs and spices in a frying pan with the stock and red wine. Cover, bring to a boil, and boil for 5 minutes. Uncover, reduce the heat slightly, and simmer until the onion is tender.

2 Add the red peppers, stir and cook until they are softened.

3 Stir in the tomatoes and capers, and simmer, uncovered, for about 30 minutes or until thickened and savory, stirring occasionally. Stir in the beans and season with salt and pepper. Simmer for a further 5-10 minutes. Remove the bay leaf before serving.

Herbed Eggplant Sauce

• • • • • • • • • • • **V** • • **Z** • • • • • • • • • • •

Makes 2 cups

If you don't like fennel and rosemary, leave them out and replace with herbs you do like: oregano and shredded basil, thyme and bay leaf, for example. Herbed Eggplant Sauce is part-stew, part-sauce, and goes particularly well with grains like couscous or bulgur.

2 eggplants,
   peeled and finely chopped
6 scallions, chopped
2 garlic cloves, crushed
1/2-1 tablespoon fennel seeds
1 tablespoon rosemary leaves,
   crumbled
pinch of crushed dried chilies

1/2 cup dry red wine
2 cups vegetable stock
4 peppers (2 yellow and 2 red,
   if possible), peeled, deseeded
   and cut into thin strips
1 14-oz can of chopped Italian
   tomatoes
1 tablespoon tomato purée
salt and freshly ground pepper

1 Put the eggplant, onions, garlic, herbs and spices, wine and 1 cup stock in a large, heavy-bottomed frying pan. Cover and boil for 5 minutes. Uncover, reduce the heat slightly, and simmer, stirring frequently, until the eggplant is tender and the liquid almost gone. Add more stock if necessary.

2 Meanwhile, put 1 cup stock and the peppers in another frying pan. stir-fry until the liquid is almost gone and the peppers are meltingly tender. Add to the eggplant mixture.

3 Stir in the tomato purée, season with salt and pepper, and simmer for 10-15 minutes or until thick and savory. Taste and adjust the seasonings. Serve with pasta or grains, as a filling for boiled potatoes or potato cases (see pages 171, 116), or use as a filling in a vegetarian lasagna.

Lentil "Bolognese" Sauce

· · · · · · · · · · · Ⓥ · · Ⓩ · · · · · · · · · ·

Makes 4 cups

This really looks like Bolognese sauce; the lentils give it a "meaty" texture, but it is not at all stodgy. Lentil Bolognese is perfect for pasta, but it makes a wonderful filling for Steam-Roasted Stuffed Mushrooms (see page 126) as well. I love it so much, I eat it straight out of the bowl (or the frying pan, if I just can't wait).

1/2 cup dry red wine
3 1/4 cups vegetable stock
   or water
8 scallions, sliced
2 dry-packed sun-dried tomatoes,
   chopped (use scissors)
2-3 black olives in brine, drained
   and flesh slivered off the stones
1-2 pinches crushed dried chilies

1/4 teaspoon dried oregano
12 garlic cloves, crushed
1/2 lb brown or green lentils, rinsed
   and picked over
2 14-oz cans of chopped
   tomatoes
salt and freshly ground pepper
vegetable bouillon powder
   (optional)

1 Put the wine, 1 cup of the stock or water, onions, sun-dried tomatoes, olive pieces, chilies, oregano and garlic in a heavy-bottomed saucepan or flameproof casserole. Bring to a boil, then reduce the heat and simmer until the liquid is almost gone.

2 Stir in the remaining stock or water (reserving about 1/4 cup), the lentils and canned tomatoes. Season with pepper and simmer for 45-60 minutes or until the lentils are tender and the sauce thick.

3 If you have used water instead of stock, add some vegetable bouillon powder at this point. At any rate, season with salt and pepper.

4 Ladle out about a third of the sauce and dilute it with the remaining 1/4 cup stock. In small batches, purée it in a blender until smooth. Combine the puréed and unpuréed sauce.

Colombian Tomato-Cheese Sauce

Makes 3 cups

Papas a la Chorreadas *is a spicy Colombian dish of boiled potatoes smothered in a creamy tomato and cheese sauce. Low-fat mozzarella is not a bad substitute for the mild white cheese of the original, and ricotta stands in for the cream. Serve with boiled potatoes or Steam-Roasted Potatoes (see page 176).*

I large onion, chopped
2 garlic cloves, crushed
I fresh chile, deseeded and
   finely chopped
I cup vegetable stock
I teaspoon ground turmeric
I teaspoon ground cumin
2 14-oz cans of tomatoes,
   drained and chopped

salt and freshly ground pepper
2-3 tablespoons chopped fresh
   cilantro
6 tablespoons ricotta cheese
   at room temperature
3 oz low-fat mozzarella
   cheese, diced

1 Put the onion, garlic, chile, stock and spices in a heavy-bottomed saucepan or frying pan. Cover and boil for 5-7 minutes. Uncover, reduce the heat, and simmer for 3-5 minutes or until the onions are tender and the stock almost gone.

2 Stir in the tomatoes and simmer for 10-15 minutes or until thick. Season with salt and pepper, stir in the cilantro and remove from the heat.

3 Stir a tablespoon of the sauce into the ricotta, then stir the ricotta mixture back into the sauce.

4 Stir in the mozzarella, return to the heat and allow to warm gently. (Don't simmer or the ricotta may separate; the mozzarella should just turn to meltingly soft lumps—if it melts too much, it becomes stringy.)

Red Pepper and Tomato Sauce

· · · · · · · · · · · **Ⓥ** · · **Ⓩ** · · · · · · · · · · ·

Makes 3 cups

Red peppers (and yellow ones, see the following recipe) make vivid sauces. Peppers are more digestible when peeled, and the texture is much improved, but there is no need to peel them for this sauce, because sieving the sauce in step 4 eliminates the pepper skins. If you want to make a Red Pepper Sauce (as opposed to a Red Pepper and Tomato Sauce), omit the chopped tomatoes and double the amount of peppers.

2 cups vegetable stock
1 large mild onion, chopped
1 garlic clove, crushed
1 tablespoon paprika
6 red peppers, deseeded
   and coarsely chopped

1 14-oz can of chopped tomatoes
salt and freshly ground pepper

1 Put half the stock, the onion, the garlic and the paprika in a heavy-bottomed frying pan. Cover and boil for 5-7 minutes. Uncover, reduce the heat and simmer, stirring occasionally, until the onions are almost tender and the liquid almost gone.

2 Stir in the peppers and the remaining stock, and simmer, uncovered, over a moderate heat for a few minutes or until the peppers are tender and the liquid greatly reduced.

3 Add the tomatoes, season with salt and pepper, and simmer, uncovered, for 15-20 minutes or until thick and savory. Leave to cool slightly.

4 Purée the sauce in small batches in a blender, then push the sauce through a sieve. Taste, and adjust the seasonings, if necessary.

Yellow Pepper Tarragon Sauce

· · · · · · · · · · · **V** · · **Z** · · · · · · · · · · · ·

Makes 1 1/2 cups

I first developed this tart, tarragon-infused yellow pepper sauce over 12 years ago, after losing 80 pounds in weight and pledging myself to a high-nutrition, lower-fat way of life. In those days, new as I was to the low-fat game, I wondered how I would survive without all those beloved fat- and oil-laden concoctions that made me enormous in the first place. Yellow Pepper Sauce, with a tarragon wine vinegar-flavored base, was my variation on the theme of Béarnaise Sauce—the tarragon-infused egg yolk-butter emulsion. Over the years, my palate has learned to hate the fatty textures of egg yolk-butter emulsions, and to love the soothing smoothness of stock-sautéed vegetable purées. I never miss Béarnaise these days, but I do crave this sauce. Serve it with Steamed Asparagus, Vegetable-Stuffed Peppers (see page 124), or Bean Cakes (see page 108).

6 large yellow peppers, deseeded
   and coarsely diced
1 cup vegetable stock
1/2 cup dry white wine
   or dry vermouth
1/4 cup tarragon wine
   vinegar

1/2 teaspoon dried tarragon,
   crumbled
pinch of cayenne
4 scallions, sliced
1 tablespoon chopped fresh
   parsley
salt and freshly ground pepper

1 Put all the ingredients in a deep, heavy-bottomed frying pan. Bring to a boil, then reduce the heat and simmer, uncovered, for 20-30 minutes or until the peppers are tender and the liquid greatly reduced. Leave to cool slightly.

2 Purée the pepper mixture in batches in a blender, then push through a sieve, rubbing the purée through with a wooden spoon. The pepper skins will be left behind; discard them.

3 Return the sauce to the pan and bring to a simmer. Taste, and adjust the seasonings, if necessary.

Terracotta Vegetable Sauce

· · · · · · · · · · · **V** · · **Z** · · · · · · · · · · ·

Makes 2 cups

Named for its color, this (like the Gravy recipe on page 94) is a good example of how vegetable purées can be used to make rich non-fat sauces. Sieving only half the sauce gives an interesting texture, but sieve the whole thing if you want it totally smooth. Serve with potatoes, steamed cauliflower, or pasta, or ladle it over rice or another grain (see pages 51, 67, 69 and 73).

1 lb mushrooms, quartered
2 onions, chopped
2 large red peppers, deseeded,
    peeled and chopped
2 garlic cloves, crushed
1 large carrot, coarsely grated
4 cups vegetable stock

1/2 cup dry white wine
2 dashes teriyaki sauce
1/2 teaspoon dried tarragon
1/2 teaspoon ground allspice
2 tablespoons tomato purée
salt and freshly ground pepper

1 Put the mushrooms, onions, peppers, garlic, carrot, 1 cup stock, wine, teriyaki sauce, tarragon and allspice in a large, heavy-bottomed frying pan. Stir to combine very well. Bring to a boil, then reduce the heat slightly and simmer briskly until the vegetables are tender and the liquid is greatly reduced and syrupy. Lower the heat and let the vegetables gently "fry" in their own juices for a few minutes, stirring occasionally.

2 Stir in the tomato purée, season with salt and pepper, and let cool slightly.

3 Purée the mixture, in small batches, in a blender or food processor until smooth. Push half the purée through a sieve, then mix the sieved sauce with the unsieved sauce. Let cool completely, then cover and refrigerate until needed.

4 To reheat, pour into a saucepan and thin, if necessary, with 2-3 tablespoons stock or water. Simmer gently, stirring occasionally.

Beans and Pulses

Due to their high protein count and their substantial, filling nature, dried beans and pulses are a vegetarian staple. Although the protein they provide is not quite complete, it is complemented by grains or animal protein (in dairy products) to give a full measure of amino acids (the building blocks of protein). But it is not merely a question of impeccable nutritional references; beans make very good eating. There is an overwhelming variety to choose from, and countless ways of preparing them, so you should never have to suffer bean boredom. And—good news for the chronically rushed—more and more different types of beans are becoming available in cans, so soaking and long simmering are not always necessary. Beans do have a reputation for windiness, but, happily, the more beans you eat, the less you will suffer from this particular affliction!

Curried Kidney Beans

Ⓥ · · Ⓩ

Makes 4 cups

This recipe is based on traditional Indian home cooking. Serve with Sweet Rice Pulao (see page 60) and Raita (see pages 191-92), or if time is at a minimum, with plain boiled rice.

1 large mild onion, coarsely chopped
1 1/2 cups vegetable stock
1/2-inch piece of fresh ginger,
  peeled and crushed
1/2 teaspoon each of ground
  cinnamon, ground coriander
  and ground cumin
pinch of ground cloves
pinch of cayenne

1 bay leaf
1 garlic clove, crushed
2 14-oz cans of tomatoes,
  drained
2 15-oz cans of kidney beans,
  drained and rinsed
salt
chopped fresh cilantro to garnish

1 Put the onion, 1 cup stock, ginger, spices, bay leaf and garlic in a heavy-bottomed frying pan. Cover and boil for 5-7 minutes. Uncover, reduce the heat, and simmer until the onions are tender and the onions and spices are frying in their own juices.

2 Crush the tomatoes with your hands and add them, with the juice from the cans, to the frying pan. Simmer for 3-4 minutes, then add the beans and remaining stock. Season with salt and simmer briskly for 15-20 minutes or until thick and savory. Taste, and adjust the seasonings if necessary. Discard the bay leaf, and serve garnished with chopped cilantro.

Red Beans and Rice

· · · · · · · · · · · **V** · · **Z** · · · · · · · · · · ·

Makes 4 cups

It is said that Louis Armstrong (Satchmo) loved the classic New Orleans (excuse me, "N'Awlins") combination of red beans and rice so much that he signed his letters "Red Beans and Ricely Yours." Because I dote on brown rice (and its nutritional profile is so high) I always serve these beans with the brown stuff; but white is more traditional.

I large mild onion, coarsely
   chopped
2 red peppers, peeled, deseeded
   and coarsely chopped
2 celery stalks, chopped
1/4 teaspoon ground cumin
1/4 teaspoon ground coriander
pinch of cayenne
1/4 teaspoon dried thyme
1/4 teaspoon dried oregano, crumbled

1/2 cup red wine
1 1/2 cup vegetable stock
1 14-oz can of chopped tomatoes
1 bay leaf
salt and freshly ground pepper
2 15-oz cans of red kidney beans,
   drained and rinsed
cooked rice (see page 51), to serve

1 Put the vegetables, spices, herbs, wine and stock in a heavy-bottomed frying pan. Cover and boil for 5-7 minutes. Uncover, reduce the heat, and simmer until the vegetables are nearly tender and frying in their own juices.

2 Stir in the tomatoes and bay leaf. Season with salt and pepper, and simmer for 5 minutes.

3 Stir in the beans and simmer for 10 minutes more, or until the mixture is thick and savory. Discard the bay leaf, and serve with rice.

Zesty Beans

· · · · · · · · · · · **V** · · **Z** · · · · · · · · · ·

Makes 2 1/2 cups

These are zesty, yet delicate. If you prefer less zest and more delicacy, leave out the chile and chili powder.

1 large mild onion, chopped
2 garlic cloves, crushed
1 fresh chile, deseeded and chopped
1/2 teaspoon dried oregano,
   crumbled
1/2 teaspoon chili powder
3/4 teaspoon ground cumin
1 cup vegetable stock
1 teaspoon Dijon mustard

1 15-oz can of cannellini beans,
   drained and rinsed
1 15-oz can of haricot blancs,
   drained and rinsed
1 14-oz can of chopped tomatoes
2 tablespoons chopped
   fresh parsley
salt
chopped fresh cilantro,
   to garnish

1 Put the onion, garlic, chile, herbs and spices in a large frying pan with the stock. Cover and boil for 5-7 minutes. Uncover, reduce the heat, and simmer until the onions are "frying" in their own juices.

2 Stir in the mustard, beans, tomatoes and parsley. Season with salt and simmer gently, stirring occasionally, for 15-20 minutes or until thick. Serve with rice or another grain, or on toast, sprinkled with chopped cilantro.

Beans on Toast

· · · · · · · · · · · · **V** · · **Z** · · · · · · · · · · ·

Makes 2 1/2 cups

Of course, you could always open a can of baked beans, and throw the contents at a slice of toast, but this is almost as quick and has quite a bit of pizzazz. I firmly believe that pizzazz is important, even on fraught days that leave no time or strength for serious cooking. Another soybean-based product, hoisin sauce is now available in most larger supermarkets.

I garlic clove, crushed
I small onion, chopped
2-3 dry-packed sun-dried tomatoes,
    finely chopped (use scissors)
    (optional)
pinch of crushed dried chilies
I cup vegetable stock
2 15-oz cans of black-eyed beans
    or red kidney beans
    drained and rinsed

1-2 tablespoons spicy ketchup
    (such as Salsa Ketchup)
I cup tomato purée
I tablespoon hoisin sauce
juice of 1/2 lime
toasted whole wheat bread

1 Put the garlic, onion, sun-dried tomatoes (if using), chile flakes and stock in a heavy-bottomed frying pan. Cover and boil for 7-10 minutes. Uncover, and simmer briskly until the onions and garlic are tender and the liquid has almost boiled away.

2 Add the beans and stir so they are thoroughly mixed with the onion mixture. Stir the remaining ingredients (except the lime juice and toast) into the beans, and simmer for 10-15 minutes, stirring in the lime juice 5 minutes before the end of the cooking time. Ladle over toasted bread to serve.

Fava Bean Corn Stew

· · · · · · · · · · · · ❷ · · · · · · · · · · · · ·

Makes 3 cups

Recipes utilizing pre-packed foods from your cupboard are marvelous for those exhausted weekday evenings when you want something hot and sustaining, but have very little patience for real cooking. All you have to do here is open a few cans and chop a few herbs. Beans and corn are a time-honored vegetarian partnership.

6 scallions, thinly sliced
3-4 dry-packed sun-dried
   tomatoes, diced (use scissors)
   (optional)
about 1 cup vegetable stock
1 14-oz can of fava beans,
   drained
1 12-oz can of corn kernels,
   drained

1 14-oz can of chopped
   tomatoes
salt and freshly ground pepper
6-7 tablespoons shredded fresh
   mint or basil, mixed with
   1/2 lb non-fat cottage cheese

1 Put the onions, sun-dried tomatoes (if using) and stock in a heavy-bottomed frying pan. Bring to a boil, then reduce the heat and simmer until the onions and tomatoes are tender.

2 Stir in the fava beans, corn and tomatoes. Season with salt and pepper, and simmer, uncovered, for about 10 minutes, then stir in 4 tablespoons of the mint. Stir the remaining mint or basil into the cottage cheese. Garnish each bowlful of stew with a dollop of the herbed cottage cheese, and serve the remainder separately in a bowl.

Ⓥ Omit the cottage cheese garnish.

Bean Cakes

· · · · · · · · · · **Ⓥ** · · **Ⓩ** · · · · · · · · · · ·

Makes about 8 cakes

I hate lumpy beanburgers, the kind that have bits of whole beans mixed in with the mashed ones. These smooth bean cakes are much more sophisticated; I especially like the contrast of the creamy bean–eggplant interior with the crisp crumb–cheese exterior. The eggplant, sponge-like, soaks up the flavors of the infusion, so that the entire bean cake is imbued with the mellow flavors of garlic and olives. Serve the cakes on one of the tomato or pepper sauces or Gravy (see pages 91-94), or accompany with Fruit-Fennel Chutney (see page 190), Mint-Cilantro Raita (see page 191) or Green Pea Dip (see page 37). The bean cakes are also delicious in pita pockets, or wrapped in tortillas, garnished with the accompaniments.

INFUSION
5 scallions, sliced
2 dry-packed sun-dried
   tomatoes, diced (use scissors)
3 black olives in brine, drained
   and flesh slivered off the stones
1/4 teaspoon dried oregano
4 oz peeled eggplant, diced
pinch of dried chile flakes
1-2 garlic cloves, crushed
1 cup vegetable stock

BEAN MIX
1 15 oz can of butter beans,
   drained and rinsed

1 tablespoon each of tomato purée,
   cottage cheese, grated Parmesan
   cheese and plain breadcrumbs
salt and freshly ground pepper
   (optional)

COATING
5 tablespoons plain breadcrumbs
2-3 tablespoons grated Parmesan
   cheese
salt and freshly ground pepper
olive oil and water spray
   (see page 5)

1 Preheat the oven to 400°F.

2 Put all the infusion ingredients in a saucepan. Bring to a boil, then reduce the heat and simmer until the eggplant is very tender and the liquid has been absorbed. Let cool.

3 Put the cooled infusion in a food processor and add the bean mix, except the salt and pepper. Process until smooth, then taste and season with salt and pepper, if necessary.

4 For the coating, mix the plain breadcrumbs with the Parmesan cheese. Season with salt and pepper, and spread on a plate. Scoop up a heaped tablespoon of the bean mixture, form it into a rough ball, and toss it in the crumbs until evenly coated. Flatten it to 1/2-inch-thick cake. Place on a non-stick baking sheet that you have lightly misted with olive oil spray. Repeat until all the bean mixture has been used.

5 Bake in the oven for 10-12 minutes, then carefully turn the cakes and bake for a further 10-12 minutes or until they are crusty and golden all over.

Eggplant Bean Stew

· · · · · · · · · · **V** · · **Z** · · · · · · · · · ·

Makes 4 cups

This is another recipe combining those natural partners, eggplants and beans, this time in a Sicilian-influenced stew. I love this ladled generously over wedges of Savory Polenta Pie with Garlic and Scallions (see page 80). Of course, polenta is typical of northern Italy, far from Sicily, both culturally and geographically, but they do go together so well. Throw gastronomic cultural correctness to the winds, and enjoy it.

4-5 black olives in brine, drained
    and flesh slivered off the stones
2 tablespoons drained capers
1-2 tablespoons raisins
2 dry-packed sun-dried tomatoes,
    diced (use scissors)
3-4 garlic cloves, crushed
4 scallions, sliced
1-2 good pinches of crushed
    dried chilies
1 cup vegetable stock
1/2 cup dry red wine
1 eggplant, about 12 oz
    peeled and diced

3 small zucchini, diced
2 14-oz cans of tomatoes,
    drained and cut into strips
salt and freshly ground pepper
1 15-oz can of white northern beans,
    drained and rinsed
2-3 tablespoons shredded
    fresh basil
4-5 tablespoons chopped
    fresh parsley

1 Put the olive pieces, capers, raisins, sun-dried tomatoes, garlic, onions, chilies, stock and wine in a large, non-reactive flameproof casserole or heavy-bottomed saucepan. Cover and boil for 5-7 minutes.

2 Add the eggplant, zucchini and tomato strips, and season with salt and pepper. Simmer, uncovered, for 10-15 minutes, then stir in the beans and herbs, and simmer, stirring occasionally, for 5-10 minutes more or until the eggplant is tender.

Black Beans

· · · · · · · · · · · **(V)** · · **(Z)** · · · · · · · · · · · ·

Makes 5 cups

Black beans can be purchased in cans or by the pound in dry form. It is a noble bean. The color is purple-black, the texture is velvety. Serve them as they are, with Mint and Cilantro Raita (see page 191) and Mexican Salsa (see page 186), or layer them with tomato sauce (see pages 91-92) and tortilla chips (see page 47), top with shredded low-fat mozzarella, and bake. If you wish, purée half the beans and mix with the unpuréed portion for an interesting texture. These beans also form the basis of Black Bean Soup (see page 13), or—with white rice.

I lb dried black beans, washed
  and picked over
6 1/2 cups water (if your water is
  very hard, use bottled water)
I large mild onion, chopped
7 1/2 cups vegetable stock

2-4 garlic cloves, crushed
1/2 teaspoon ground cumin
pinch of ground cloves
1/4 teaspoon ground allspice
1/2 teaspoon ground coriander
1-2 pinches cayenne
salt and freshly ground pepper

I Put the beans in a large bowl, cover with water, and let soak overnight in a cool place. Next day, drain them, discarding the water.

2 Put the onion, 1 cup stock, garlic and all the spices in a heavy-bottomed saucepan. Cover and boil for 5-7 minutes. Uncover, reduce the heat, and simmer, stirring occasionally, until the onions and spices are frying in their own juices. When the onions are tender, stir in the drained beans.

3 Stir in the remaining 6 1/2 cups of stock, cover and boil hard for 10 minutes. Skim off the foam, then reduce the heat and simmer, partially covered, for 1 1/2 hours.

4 Season with salt and pepper and simmer for a further 1 hour or until very tender. Taste and adjust the seasonings.

Pink Lentils

· · · · · · · · · · **V** · · **Z** · · · · · · · · · ·

Makes 2 1/2 cups

Pink lentils are suddenly very fashionable, which is fine with me; the more fashionable they become, the easier they are to find in supermarkets and health food stores. They cook very quickly and have an earthy taste, as do all lentils, but have a delicate earthiness, if you can imagine such a thing. I'm always delighted when a truly useful, basic and healthful food hits "fad" status. Like sun-dried tomatoes, pink lentils deserve their current popularity, and—like sun-dried tomatoes—I hope they are here to stay.

about 5 cups vegetable stock
   or water
2 dry-packed sun-dried
   tomatoes, chopped
   (use scissors)
2 garlic cloves, crushed
6 scallions, sliced

pinch of crushed dried chilies
3 black olives in brine, drained
   and flesh slivered off the stones
9 oz pink lentils, rinsed
freshly ground pepper
salt and vegetable bouillon powder
   (optional)

1 Put 1/2 cup stock or water in a heavy-bottomed saucepan with the tomatoes, garlic, scallions, chilies and olive pieces. Bring to a boil, then reduce the heat and simmer until the liquid is almost gone.

2 Stir in the lentils and season with pepper. Stir in 4 cups of the remaining stock and boil for 10 minutes. Reduce the heat and simmer, partially covered, for 30-35 minutes or until the lentils are tender. Add a bit more stock or water during this time, if necessary, to prevent scorching. If you have used water instead of stock, add some vegetable bouillon powder and salt.

HOW TO LOVE YOUR LIVER

If these lentils are cooled and then puréed in a food processor, they look startlingly like liver pâté. It spreads like liver pâté too, but the taste is pure, earthy pink lentils. Quite wonderful, really.

Green Split Pea Dhal

· · · · · · · · · · **(V)** · · **(Z)** · · · · · · · · · ·

Makes 3 1/2 cups

A dhal is a kind of sauce made from cooked pulses, meant to accompany curry dishes. Serve this—along with chutneys and Raita (see pages 191-92)—with any of the vegetable curries and Sweet Rice Pulao (see page 60). The combination of tastes and textures, as well as excellent nutrition, makes a meal that is hard to beat.

3 cups vegetable stock
   or water
1/2-inch piece of ginger,
   peeled and grated
2 small onions, diced
2 garlic cloves, crushed
1 fresh green chile, deseeded
   and finely chopped
1/2 teaspoon ground turmeric

1 1/2 teaspoons ground coriander
1 teaspoon ground cumin
1 teaspoon mustard powder
1 14-oz can of tomatoes,
   drained and chopped
1/2 lb dried green split peas,
   rinsed and picked over
salt
1 teaspoon garam masala

1 Put 1 cup stock or water in a heavy-bottomed saucepan with the ginger, onions, garlic, chile and spices. Cover and boil for 5-7 minutes. Uncover, reduce the heat, and simmer, stirring occasionally, until the onions are tender, and the onions and spices are frying in their own juices.

2 Stir in the tomatoes and cook for 1 minute. Stir in the split peas and remaining stock or water, and simmer, covered, for 35-45 minutes or until the peas are tender and the consistency is that of a thick sauce. Season with salt (and some vegetable bouillon powder, if you have used water instead of stock) during the last 10-15 minutes of cooking.

3 When the peas are done, stir in the garam masala. This dhal can be reheated, but it will have thickened. Thin with stock or water as necessary.

Vegetables

An inspiring, life-enhancing selection of vegetables should be the heart of *any* healthy diet, not just a vegetarian one. Wander up and down the fresh produce section of your local supermarket and revel in the bounty: glossy purple eggplants; jewel-like red, yellow and orange peppers; huge posies of cauliflower curving out of their greens like virginal bouquets for vegetarian brides; sweet potatoes, salad potatoes, baking potatoes, all-purpose potatoes—an orgy of starchy comfort; thorny artichokes; thrusting asparagus; tomatoes that may actually taste like tomatoes; cabbages of all hues, curly and straight…it drives one wild with meal possibilities! And it's not just the sheer gastronomic joy of all this vegetable overflow; the health benefits cannot be overstated. Vegetables are *profoundly* important to your general health and well-being.

Vegetables high in beta-carotene (your body uses beta-carotene to make vitamin A) are believed to give protection against the development of cancers affecting the skin and lining tissues (such as lung and breast cancers), bladder and digestive-tract cancers, and prostate and cervical cancers. Such vegetables include asparagus, beets, broccoli, carrots, red and yellow peppers, dark green leaves (such as spinach, chard and watercress), tomatoes and corn.

Another vegetable group believed to protect against cancer is the brassica (cabbage) family, including brussels sprouts, cabbage, cauliflower, broccoli and kohlrabi. Large and frequent servings may help reduce the risk of cancers of the stomach and large intestine.

Virtually all vegetables are bursting with important vitamins and fiber, they fill you up, they keep your digestive system working nicely, and they provide much pleasure. Snack on them, dine on them, eat as many different kinds, in as many combinations, as you can. If you have little time for peeling, scraping, slicing and dicing, try frozen vegetables—they are nearly as nutritious as fresh (unless you are in the habit of yanking them out of the soil and cooking them on the spot—*nothing* compares to that!).

Stuffed Stuff

Filled vegetable cases make a wonderful focus for a meal. Served with a sauce (present them on a bed of sauce, rather than smothered with it) and a salad or interesting side vegetable, they are filling, satisfying and attractive. All sorts of vegetables can be stuffed: potatoes, cabbage leaves, winter squash, zucchini: let your imagination be your guide. The following recipes and techniques should get you started in the stuffing game—multiply or divide the recipes to suit the number of those you are feeding, and their appetites.

Potato Cases

· · · · · · · · · · · · **V** · · **Z** · · · · · · · · · · · ·

These potato skins turn crunchy, like chips, and are meant to be filled with something wonderful: mushroom ragout, vegetable curry or chili, Lentil bolognese, or even mashed potatoes (cook the scooped out centers, mash with a dab of cottage cheese and grated low-fat cheese, and use to fill the cases).

large baking potatoes

1 Preheat the oven to 400°F.

2 Scrub the potatoes, and halve them lengthwise.

3 With a teaspoon or melon baller, scoop out the insides of the potatoes, leaving a shell about 1/4-inch thick. Save the scraps for another use (see box).

4 Bake directly in the oven for 25-35 minutes or until golden brown and very crisp. Serve at once, filled with a savory mixture (see above).

POTATO GRATIN

Don't throw the potato insides away. Use them to make this starchy and satisfying gratin:

1 Scoop the insides of the potatoes straight into a saucepan and add enough stock to cover. Season with salt and plenty of pepper, and a little grated nutmeg or a pinch each of ground cumin and cayenne. Bring to a boil, then reduce the heat and simmer, covered, until the potato is tender. Do not drain.

2 Mash roughly (just to break up the pieces, not to purée them) in the saucepan with a potato masher, then spread in a gratin dish. Dribble on a little skim milk and sprinkle with some grated Parmesan or low-fat cheddar or Swiss cheese. Place under the broiler until bubbly and well browned on top.

Squash Cases

· · · · · · · · · · · · · · **V** · · · · · · · · · · · ·

Acorn squash and butternut squash, two of the hard-shelled winter squashes, are now available during the autumn in many supermarkets. Butternut squash has a butterscotch-colored shell and is shaped like a gourd; acorn squash is round, ribbed, and green with orange highlights. Both, when baked, have sweet, tender, mouthfilling flesh and make excellent cases for all sorts of rice dishes or bean- and vegetable-based purées and stews. A butternut squash has a small cavity, while an acorn squash has a large one.

To bake either of the squashes, preheat the oven to 400°F. Halve them from stem to stern, and scrape out the seeds and fibers. Place the pieces, cavity-up, on a baking sheet, and mist lightly with oil and water spray (see page 5). Bake in the oven for 35-45 minutes (the timing depends on the size of the squash). The idea is to bake them long enough for the flesh to become very tender, but not so long that the squash loses its shape and collapses. Fill the cavity with any rice or vegetable mixture you like. The gorgeous yellow/orange flesh of butternut squash, and its voluptuous texture and sweet flavor, work particularly well with Sweet Rice Pulao (see page 60). Serve the rice-stuffed squash on a bed of Pepper Sauce (see page 99) or surrounded by a wreath of Stir-Fried Peppers (see page 151). Mushroom Ragout (see page 167) is especially good heaped to overflowing in a baked acorn squash half. The vegetable curry mixtures (see pages 158-62) are also very good in both squashes.

Cabbage Parcels

· · · · · · · · · · · · **Ⓥ** · · · · · · · · · · · ·

Makes 12–15

This is easy to make, but it is fairly labor-intensive—all that peeling, chopping, dicing, steaming and rolling. For those who enjoy kitchen activity, the preparation is as pleasurable as the eating; those in a constant rush will—no doubt—recoil in horror. These Cabbage Parcels can be made a day or so in advance—indeed the flavor improves after a day or two.

1 large Savoy cabbage	3 dry-packed sun-dried tomatoes,
2 zucchini, chopped	chopped (use scissors)
1 eggplant, peeled and chopped	pinch of crushed dried chilies
2 large carrots, chopped	3 black olives in brine, drained
2 peppers (1 red, 1 yellow),	and flesh slivered off the stones
peeled, deseeded and chopped	1/2 cup dry red wine
8 scallions, sliced	1 tablespoon tomato purée
2 garlic cloves, crushed	6 tablespoons chopped fresh parsley
1 tablespoon paprika	salt and freshly ground pepper
1 1/2 cups vegetable stock	2 cups tomato purée

1 Cut the core out of the bottom of the cabbage. Remove the tough outer leaves (save them for garnish), and pull off 12-15 leaves (you will have some bigger and some smaller ones—that's fine). Set aside the heart of the cabbage. With a sharp paring knife, pare down the tough central vein on each leaf. Steam the leaves over boiling water for 5-7 minutes or until they are flexible and almost tender. Refresh under cold running water to stop further cooking, drain well, and set aside. Chop up the cabbage heart, and set aside.

2 Preheat the oven to 400°F.

3 Put the zucchini, eggplant, carrots, peppers, onions, garlic, paprika, 1 cup of the stock, the sun-dried tomatoes, chile, olive pieces and red wine in a large, heavy-bottomed frying pan. Cover and boil for 5-7 minutes. Uncover, reduce the heat and simmer for 5-10 minutes more or until the vegetables are tender and the liquid is almost gone. Stir in 1 tablespoon of the tomato purée and 4 tablespoons chopped parsley, and season with salt and pepper. Leave to cool.

4 Lay a cabbage leaf out flat on your work surface. Put 1-2 tablespoons of the vegetable mixture on one end of the leaf. Tuck in the end and the sides, and roll to make a neat parcel. Place, seam-side down, on a plate. Repeat until all the leaves are filled. There will be some leftover filling; set it aside.

5 Combine the chopped cabbage heart and remaining 1/2 cup stock in a frying pan. Stir-fry until the cabbage is tender and the liquid almost gone. Stir in the leftover vegetable stuffing, the 2 cups of tomato purée and remaining parsley. Simmer for 5 minutes, then season with salt and pepper.

6 Choose a baking dish that will hold the cabbage parcels in one snug layer. Spoon some sauce onto the bottom of the dish, then carefully arrange the cabbage rolls in the dish, seam-side down. Pour the remaining sauce over the parcels. Cover the dish and bake in the oven for 30-40 minutes or until hot and bubbling.

7 To serve, line a platter with the reserved outer cabbage leaves. Lift out the cabbage rolls (gently shaking off the sauce) and place on the leaves. Pour the sauce into a sauceboat and serve separately. Serve with mashed potatoes, kasha (see page 73) or couscous (see page 69).

Stuffed Eggplant

· · · · · · · · · · **V** · · **Z** · · · · · · · · · · ·

Makes 2 stuffed halves

I use cremini mushrooms to stuff eggplant halves, because they result in a dark stuffing. The almost-black mushroom stuffing contained in the dark purple eggplant case, set against the scarlet sauce, is a dramatic sight. It tastes good, too. Serve one or two halves per person.

I eggplant, 10-12 oz
oil and water spray (see page 5)
I garlic clove, crushed
1/4 lb cremini mushrooms,
  finely chopped
1/2 cup red wine

1/4 cup vegetable stock
3 tablespoons chopped fresh
  parsley
salt and freshly ground pepper
Tomato or Red Pepper Sauce
  (see pages 91-92 and 99),
  to serve

I Preheat the oven to 450°F.

2 Trim the stem from the eggplant and cut the eggplant in half lengthwise. With a sharp knife, cut out the center of each eggplant half, about 1/4 inch from the edge, but replace the meat from the interior in the eggplant half. Cut almost down to the skin, but be careful not to cut through the skin. Mist the cut surfaces of the eggplant with oil spray.

3 Choose a baking dish that will hold the eggplant halves side by side. Put a few spoonfuls of water in the dish and place the eggplant halves in it, cut sides down. Bake in the oven for 10-15 minutes or until the eggplant is partially tender. Cool slightly.

4 Remove the flesh from each eggplant half, leaving a shell of about 1/4-inch thickness. The shell will most likely lie flat; don't worry.

5 Chop the baked eggplant flesh and combine it in a heavy-bottomed frying pan with the garlic, mushrooms, wine and stock. Sauté, stirring occasionally, until the mixture is very dark, the liquid almost gone, and the mushrooms tender. Stir in 2 tablespoons chopped parsley and season with salt and pepper.

6 Spoon the mushroom mixture in a strip down the center of each eggplant shell. Mold the shell around the filling into a boat shape. Lightly mist with oil and water spray a baking dish that will hold the stuffed shells snugly. Put the stuffed eggplants in the dish and bake, uncovered in the oven, for 15-20 minutes or until sizzling and heated through. Serve on a bed of Quick Tomato or Red Pepper Sauce. Sprinkle with the remaining chopped parsley.

GARLIC TIP

To remove the smell of raw garlic from your fingers, wash your hands first, then rub your fingers against the bowl of a stainless steel spoon, under cold running water. Wash your hands once more and the smell will be gone.

Stuffed Zucchini

. . . . **Z** . . . .

Makes 4 stuffed halves

Zucchini seems to be made for stuffing; hollowed out they form perfect little boat shapes. The chopped-up zucchini flesh marries well with Italian seasonings.

2 medium zucchini
I small onion, chopped
I garlic clove, crushed
2 dry-packed sun-dried tomatoes, chopped (use scissors)
2 black olives in brine, drained and flesh slivered off the stones
pinch of crushed dried chilies
1/2-1 cup vegetable stock
1/4 cup dry vermouth
4 tablespoons cooked brown rice (see page 51)

freshly ground pepper
2-3 tablespoons grated Parmesan cheese
2 tablespoons chopped fresh parsley
2 tablespoons shredded fresh basil or mint
olive oil and water spray (see page 5)
lemon wedges or Red Pepper or Quick Tomato Sauce (see pages 99 and 91-92), to serve

I Preheat the oven to 450°F.

2 Trim the zucchini and halve lengthwise. With a teaspoon, hollow out each half, leaving a shell about 1/2-inch thick. Chop the scooped-out flesh, and put in a heavy-bottomed frying pan with the onion, garlic, sun-dried tomatoes, olive pieces, chilies, 1/2 cup stock and vermouth. Bring to the boil, and boil uncovered, for 5-7 minutes, stirring occasionally until the onions are tender and the liquid almost gone. Stir in the rice and a spoonful or so of extra stock, if necessary. Season with pepper and stir until everything is well combined and the rice is imbued with the taste of the onion-garlic mixture. Remove from the heat, and stir in most of the cheese and the herbs.

3 While the filling is cooking, steam the zucchini shells over boiling water for 3-5 minutes or until *barely* tender. Refresh under cold running water to stop further cooking and set the color. Dry with paper towels.

4 Choose a baking dish that will hold the zucchini in one layer, and mist it with oil and water spray. Heap the rice mixture into the zucchini halves and arrange them in a baking dish. Sprinkle each with a little of the remaining cheese and bake in the oven for 15-20 minutes or until they are sizzling and the cheese has melted. Serve at once, with lemon wedges or on a bed of Red Pepper or Tomato Sauce.

Vegetable-Stuffed Peppers

· · · · · · · · · · **V** · · **Z** · · · · · · · · · · · ·

Makes 6 halves

Vegetarian dishes are either very brown (all those grains and beans) or intoxicatingly colorful (all those gorgeous vegetables). The most gorgeous of them all, of course, is the pepper, and here it is used to advantage. Stuff red peppers with a colorful mixture of gently curried shredded roots and set them on a purée of yellow peppers. Edible technicolor is the result.

3 red peppers
   several dashes of teriyaki sauce
1/2 cup, plus 2-3 tablespoons
   vegetable stock
1/2 cup dry sherry
2 carrots, coarsely grated
2 small white turnips, grated
2 small parsnips, grated
2 tablespoons raisins
1/4 teaspoon each garam
   masala, ground cumin and
   ground turmeric

6 tablespoons cooked brown
   rice (see page 51)
salt and freshly ground pepper
Yellow Pepper Sauce (follow the
   recipe on page 100 but omit
   the tarragon and use plain wine
   to serve)
chopped fresh parsley and
   cilantro, to garnish

1 Preheat the oven to 350°F.

2 Halve the peppers and remove the seeds, ribs and stems. With a swivel-bladed peeler, carefully peel each half. Steam over boiling water for 5-7 minutes or until "crisp-tender." Refresh under cold running water to prevent further cooking, and blot dry with paper towels.

3 Put the teriyaki sauce, 1/2 cup of stock, the sherry, grated vegetables, raisins and spices in a heavy-bottomed frying pan. Cook gently, stirring and tossing the vegetables until they are tender but not at all mushy, and the liquid is almost gone. Stir in the rice and season with salt and pepper.

4 Pour 2-3 tablespoons stock into a baking dish that will hold the pepper halves in one layer. Arrange the peppers in the dish, cut sides up. Spoon the vegetable mixture into the peppers. Cover the dish and bake in the oven for 30 minutes.

5 To serve, set the pepper halves on a bed of Yellow Pepper Sauce, and sprinkle with the fresh herbs.

Steam-Roasted Stuffed Mushrooms

· · · · · · · · · · · · · **Z** · · · · · · · · · · · ·

Large fresh mushrooms, stuffed or unstuffed, can be wrapped in parchment paper and roasted in a hot oven. As they roast, steam forms in the parchment parcel (it puffs up dramatically) and the mushrooms take on a succulent texture. The first time you try this should be a trial run to test your oven's performance: make a note of the baking time so that you do not have to guess next time.

large brown or white mushrooms
salt and freshly ground pepper
grated Parmesan cheese (optional)
olive oil and water spray
  (see page 5)

Rice with Scallions and
  Vermouth (see page 55)
Spicy Bean Dip (see page 42)
Spinach Filling (see page 56)
Duxelles (see page 36)

FILLING
Lentil "Bolognese" Sauce (see page 97)

1 Preheat the oven to 400°F.

2 Cut the stems out of the mushrooms. (Don't throw them away: chop them and sauté in stock, sherry and soy sauce, see page 5, or use in Duxelles or Mushroom Ragout, see pages 36 and 167.) With a teaspoon, hollow out the mushrooms slightly so that they will hold a stuffing nicely. Season them lightly with salt and pepper.

3 If you are using Lentil "Bolognese" Sauce, Spicy Bean Dip or Duxelles, stir in 1-2 tablespoons grated Parmesan if you wish. Fill each mushroom with your chosen filling, mounding it nicely. If you wish, sprinkle a bit more Parmesan on top.

4 Tear off a piece of baking parchment that will generously enfold two of the stuffed mushrooms. Fold the paper in half and crease it along the fold. Open and mist the paper lightly and evenly with oil and water spray. Place two mushrooms, evenly spaced, stuffing-side up, on one half of the parchment. Fold over the other half, and seal securely by folding over and crimping the edges all round, resulting in a roughly semi-circular parcel. The parcel should be roomy, but well sealed. Repeat for the remaining mushrooms. Slide the parcels onto a baking sheet, take to the oven and slide off the sheet, directly on the oven shelf. Bake for 25-35 minutes. The parcels will darken and puff up, and the aroma will be quite wonderful.

5 When done, slide the parcels back onto the baking sheet and take to the table. With scissors, cut a cross in the top of each packet. Carefully, with a broad spatula, lift the mushrooms onto a platter. Serve at once.

V Omit the optional Parmesan cheese.

Steam-Roasted Unstuffed Mushrooms

· · · · · · · · · · **Ⓥ** · · **Ⓩ** · · · · · · · · · ·

large brown or white mushrooms
olive oil and water spray (see
    page 5)
chopped fresh parsley
grated orange zest
finely chopped fresh garlic

dry sherry
fresh orange juice
soy sauce or teriyaki sauce
freshly ground black pepper

1 Preheat the oven to 400°F.

2 Cut the stems off the mushrooms. (Don't throw them away: use them as suggested on page 126.) With a teaspoon, hollow out the mushrooms slightly.

3 Tear a piece of parchment paper large enough to contain two of the mushrooms in one layer. Fold the paper in half and crease it along the fold. Open and mist the paper lightly and evenly with oil and water spray. Place two mushrooms, evenly spaced, stem-side up, on one half of the parchment. Scatter on the mushrooms 1 tablespoon chopped parsley, a little orange zest and 1 clove of finely chopped garlic. Sprinkle on 1 tablespoon dry sherry and 1 tablespoon orange juice, shake on a modest dash or two of soy or teriyaki sauce, and grind on pepper to taste.

4 Fold the other half of the paper over and seal securely (as described on page 127). The parcel should be roomy, but well sealed. Repeat for the remaining mushrooms. Slide the parcels onto a baking sheet, take to the oven and slide off the sheet, directly on the oven shelf. Bake for 25-35 minutes. The parcels will darken and puff up.

5 When done, slide the parcels back onto the baking sheet and take to the table. With scissors, cut a cross in the top of each packet. Carefully, with a broad spatula, lift the mushrooms onto a platter. Serve at once.

Grilled Vegetables

Grilling is an excellent treatment for eggplants, zucchini and peppers. They have a supple meatiness when grilled and are useful in all sorts of sustaining main dishes. As with many of the basic ingredients in this book, it makes sense to prepare a batch of grilled vegetables once a week and store them in the refrigerator, so they are ready for quick meals when you want them.

Grilled Eggplant

· · · · · · · · · · · **V** · · **Z** · · · · · · · · · · · ·

The usual method for preparing eggplant is to slice, salt to disgorge any bitterness, dry and then pan-fry the slices in a generous amount of olive oil. The eggplant soaks up the oil like a sponge so that—even though the eggplant itself has minimal calories and no fat—the oil-soaked slices add hundreds of fat calories to a dish. Grilling is an alternative, and with the eggplants available these days there is no bitterness, therefore no need to salt the slices first.

I eggplant, cut across into 1/4-inch slices	olive oil and water spray (see page 5)

1 Preheat the grill to the highest setting. Lightly mist a non-stick baking sheet with olive oil spray.

2 Spread out the eggplant slices in one layer on the baking sheet. *Lightly* spray the slices. Broil close to the heat, for about 5 minutes or until they are tender and speckled with brown. Turn, mist *very* lightly with oil spray and broil for a moment or so on the second side.

Grilled Zucchini

· · · · · · · · · · **V** · · **Z** · · · · · · · · · ·

Zucchini can be sliced and grilled in exactly the same way as eggplant.

olive oil and water spray (see
  page 5)

5 medium zucchini, cut
  on the slant into 1/4-inch slices

1 Preheat the grill to the highest setting. Lightly mist a non-stick baking sheet with olive oil and water spray.

2 Spread the zucchini slices in one layer on the baking sheet. *Lightly* mist the slices with the spray. Broil, close to the heat, for 35 minutes or until the slices are tender and speckled with brown. Turn, mist *lightly* with spray, and broil for a moment or two on the second side.

Smoky Ratatouille

· · · · · · · · · · **V** · · **Z** · · · · · · · · · ·

With a cache of mixed grilled vegetables in the fridge, you will be able to make a panful of rich, smoky ratatouille. Cut grilled eggplant slices and grilled zucchini slices in half, and cut grilled peppers into strips. Stir them all into Tomato Sauce (see pages 91-92) in a saucepan. Add a handful of chopped fresh herbs, and simmer for 10-15 minutes. If you wish, spread the ratatouille in a rice crust (see page 56), top with some shreds of half-fat mozzarella, and flash under the grill to melt the cheese.

Grilled Peppers

· · · · · · · · · · **V** · · **Z** · · · · · · · · · · ·

Makes 6 halves

When grilling peppers, the point is to char them—either directly over the gas burner, or under the grill. The burnt, blistered skin will turn quite black. When the burnt skin is stripped off, the pepper flesh below is tender and supple, smoky and sweet, and an exhilarating red (or yellow). Keep the grilled peppers covered on a plate in the fridge: they will render delicious juices that should never be wasted. Red and yellow peppers give the sweetest results. Grilled green peppers are good too, but they have a slightly bitter "herbal" flavor.

1 If you have a gas stove, grill the peppers by placing them directly on the flame of the gas ring. As the peppers blacken and char, turn them with tongs. Alternatively, cut them in half, "break" them slightly (by bending) so they lie flat, and place under the (gas or electric) grill, cut sides down. Grill until they blacken and char. I do mean *blackened* and *charred.* They will look awful but that is exactly how they should look. As the owner of the Carnegie Deli in New York told me years ago, *"Burning* is the secret to this kind of cooking!"

2 When blackened and charred, put the hot peppers in a plastic food bag, fold over to close the bag and leave it for at least 5-10 minutes. (They can stay in the bags much longer if necessary.) Steam will form between the charred skin and the flesh, making peeling much easier. Strip off the charred skin and discard it. (Don't rinse them in water — you will only wash away the lovely smoky flavor.) Discard the cores, seeds and stems. Save any of the juices that have accumulated in the plastic bags, to use with the peppers.

DESERT ISLAND SANDWICH

I was once asked to describe my Desert Island Dish, and I didn't hesitate for even a moment. It is a sandwich. Imagine this: Roast a garlic bulb until it turns creamy and mellow (see page 136), and spread it on a crusty slice of rustic bread. Add some grilled eggplant slices, and strips of grilled red pepper, and drizzle with the pepper juices. Top with a few slices of juicy, flavorful ripe tomato. Cover with more beautifully crusty bread and press down. Take a big bite. Crumbs on bare bosom (this is a desert island after all!), juices down chin, sunlight and sea all around, no one to object to the after-effects of all that garlic . . . When do I leave?

QUICK PIZZA

If you can find prepared pizza rounds (or raw dough in the refrigerator section at the supermarket), you can make grilled vegetable pizza in minutes:

1 Preheat the oven to 400°F.

2 Flatten the dough into four small rounds and place them, well spaced, on a non-stick baking sheet. Spread a little tomato sauce on each, top with strips of grilled eggplant, pepper and zucchini, sprinkle with low-fat mozzarella, grind on some pepper, and bake in the oven until done. If the dough is raw, make sure it is baked through, perhaps 15 minutes. If the pizza is already baked, all you need to do is heat everything and melt the cheese topping. Garnish with basil leaves and eat with gusto!

Grilled Vegetable Mosaic

· · · · · · · · · · · · · Ⓥ · · · · · · · · · · · · ·

Top an arrangement of grilled vegetables with an infusion of olives, garlic, balsamic vinegar and wine for a colorful main dish. Serve plenty of crusty bread to mop up the juices.

grilled red or yellow pepper
  halves (see page 131)
grilled zucchini slices
  (see page 130)
grilled eggplant slices
  (see page 129)
10 scallions, thinly sliced
3 black olives in brine, drained
  and flesh slivered off the stones

pinch of crushed dried chilies
1/2 tablespoon balsamic vinegar
2-4 garlic cloves, crushed
2 tablespoons dry red wine
  or dry white vermouth
2 cups vegetable stock
chopped fresh parsley
shredded fresh basil or mint

1 Arrange the grilled pepper halves, zucchini slices and eggplant slices on an attractive platter. Take your time, and make the platter of arranged vegetables look like a stunning mosaic. Drizzle on any accumulated pepper juices.

2 Put all the remaining ingredients, except the herbs, in a heavy-bottomed frying pan. Cover and bring to the boil, then reduce the heat, and simmer for 7-10 minutes. Uncover and simmer briskly until the onions are tender and the liquid is reduced and syrupy. Pour and scrape the mixture over the grilled vegetables. Scatter the herbs over the platter.

Cheese-and-Crumb-Grilled Eggplants and Zucchini

· · · · · · · · · · · · **Ⓥ** · · · · · · · · · · · ·

Serves 2-3

I was visiting friends at Lake Winnipesaukee (wonderful name, wonderful place), New Hampshire, one summer (almost 30 years ago) when everyone was talking about a new way to grill fish: dip the fillets in a jar of mayonnaise, then dredge in crumbs, and grill. The mayo keeps the fish moist and succulent. Use lengthwise slices of eggplant and zucchini instead of fish, use a low-fat mayonnaise and you have a show-stopping dish. The coating becomes crisp and delicious, and the texture of the vegetables— especially the eggplant—is quite wonderful. Why not try this with Spicy Oven-Fried Potatoes (see page 175), Green Pea Dip (see page 37), and a bit of lemon juice or balsamic vinegar.

NOTE

If you cannot find low-fat mayonnaise dressing, make your own. Whisk together 1 tablespoon French dark mustard with 1 tablespoon balsamic vinegar. Whisk in 1 16-oz carton fat-free cottage cheese and store in the fridge until needed.

97 percent fat-free mayonnaise
10-12 tablespoons breadcrumbs
4-5 tablespoons grated
   Parmesan cheese
salt and freshly ground pepper
1 long eggplant

1 long zucchini
olive oil and water spray
   (see page 5)
lemon wedges or balsamic vinegar,
   to serve (optional)

1 Preheat the grill to its highest setting.

2 Spread some mayonnaise on a large plate. Put the breadcrumbs and 1-2 tablespoons of cheese on a second large plate. Season with salt and pepper (you won't need much salt; both the cheese and the mayonnaise contain plenty), and mix well.

3 Trim the ends off the eggplant and zucchini. Peel them both. Cut the eggplant and zucchini lengthwise into slices about 1/4-inch thick.

4 Lightly mist two non-stick baking sheets with the olive oil spray.

5 Use a rubber spatula to spread mayonnaise evenly on each side of the vegetable slices, then dip the slices in the crumb and cheese mixture. Make sure both sides are well coated. Add more mayonnaise, crumbs and cheese to the plates, as needed. As the vegetable slices are done, place them on baking sheets. When they are all on the sheets, *lightly* mist the slices with olive oil spray. Position one of the baking sheets 5 inches from the broiler and cook for 3-5 minutes on each side until nicely speckled with brown. (When the first side is speckled with brown, *carefully* ease a palette knife or spatula under each slice and flip it over. If part of the breadcrumbing on the underside is disturbed, sprinkle a little more crumb and cheese mixture on before sliding the baking sheet back under the grill.) Repeat with the second baking sheet.

Serve hot or cold, with lemon wedges or balsamic vinegar, if desired.

VARIATION
Zucchini and Eggplant Parmesan

1 Grill the eggplant and zucchini slices as above. Leave them on the baking sheets.

2 Gently spread some tomato sauce (see pages 91-92) on each slice, then top with some shredded low-fat mozzarella and a little grated Parmesan. Sprinkle with a pinch of crumbled dried oregano and grind on some pepper. Flash under the grill, to melt the cheese.

Foil-Roasted Vegetables

Roasting in foil (or, for mild onions, on a nest of foil) is another useful technique, this time for roots and bulbs. Foil-roasted garlic, in particular, is a revelation: who would guess that vulgar, rambunctious garlic could turn into a mellow, sweet pussycat of a vegetable?

Baked Garlic

· · · · · · · · · · · **Ⓥ** · · · · · · · · · · · ·

Garlic, baked whole, becomes mild and unobjectionable, and the cloves soften into a kind of purée. For this technique, buy only large, firm heads of garlic, with no sprouts and no withered cloves. Store the garlic in a ventilated basket or pierced crock in a cool part of the kitchen. (Don't refrigerate, or the bulbs will begin to sprout. And don't hold on to the garlic for months, waiting until you gather enough courage to do the deed. Baked ancient garlic is revolting.) Baked fresh, firm heads of garlic are pure pleasure. Stir the resulting purée into low-fat cottage cheese or yogurt, or whirl in the processor with silken tofu to make a garlic dip or dressing. Alternatively, use it to season sauces and enrich stews and casseroles, to mash into potatoes, or to spread on bread.

large heads of firm, unblemished,
    unsprouting garlic

1 Preheat the oven to 375°F.

2 Remove the papery outer covering of the whole garlic heads, but do not separate the cloves or peel them. Place each whole head of garlic on a square of foil (shiny side of the foil facing in). Fold up the foil and crimp so that the garlic is wrapped in a roomy, tightly sealed pouch.

3 Bake in the oven for about 1 hour (timing depends on your oven and the size of the garlic bulb).

4 Remove from the oven, unwrap and cool for at least 5 minutes. Gently separate the cloves and squeeze each one over a fine-mesh sieve so that the softened garlic pops into the sieve.

5 With a wooden spoon or spatula, rub the garlic through the sieve into a small container or bowl. If you are in a hurry, forget the sieve, simply squeeze the garlic into the bowl, and push it into a mound with a rubber spatula. Cover tightly with plastic wrap and refrigerate until the purée is needed.

GARLIC IS GOOD FOR YOU

Not only is garlic a culinary gem, but it is also believed to have significant health benefits. There are many studies in medical literature implicating garlic as an agent in cholesterol and blood pressure control, and as an antibacterial, antifungal, and possibly anticarcinogenic agent. Judging from the majority of evidence, it's natural garlic—smell and all—that has therapeutic properties.

Baked Onion

· · · · · · · · · · · · Ⓥ · · · · · · · · · · · ·

There are few things sweeter than a baked onion. Eat it cut into quarters and sprinkled with balsamic vinegar, or purée it in a blender and stir into mashed potatoes or puréed root vegetables.

large mild, white onions
freshly ground pepper and
    lemon juice, to serve

1 Preheat the oven to 400°F.

2 Put the onions on a double sheet of foil, shiny side out, on a baking sheet, but do not wrap them. Bake in the oven for 1 1/4 hours or until very soft and almost collapsed.

3 With a sharp knife, cut off the stem and root ends of the onions. Remove and discard the blackened skin and first layer of each one. Serve the onions as they are, with pepper and lemon juice, or put them in a blender and purée for use in other recipes.

Baked Beets

· · · · · · · · · · · · **V** · · · · · · · · · · · · ·

Beets are a dark, earthy red, with a deep earthy taste—at their best purchased raw, wrapped in foil and baked. Baked beet makes a wonderful dip or spread: cut it into chunks and place in a blender or food processor with a spoonful or two of low-fat cottage cheese or yogurt, a splash of lemon juice or good wine vinegar, and a bit of raw garlic (or baked garlic purée, see page 136), if you wish. Season with salt and pepper, and process to a rough, chunky purée. Add more cottage cheese, lemon juice or wine vinegar and seasonings, as needed. The color, texture and taste make this a knock-out. Baked beet is excellent as well sliced and dressed with a mixture of balsamic vinegar, lime and orange juice, or with cottage cheese mixed with chopped fresh herbs.

medium-sized raw beets

1 Preheat the oven to 400°F.

2 Trim the beet greens away, scrub and wrap the whole, unpeeled beets in foil, shiny side in (3-4 beets may go in one package).

3 Bake in the oven for 1-2 hours or until tender. (Timing depends on the age and size of the beets.) Use a skewer to test if the beets are done. The skewer should go in easily but the beets should not be mushy. Leave to cool, then trim and slip off the skins.

Foil-Roasted Root Vegetables

· · · · · · · · · · · · · **Ⓥ** · · · · · · · · · · · · ·

Roasting root vegetables in this manner brings out their natural sweetness and flavor as does no other method. This technique works for rutabagas, turnips, celery root, carrots and parsnips. The baked vegetables may be served as they are, or mashed and whipped with buttermilk or cottage cheese, or mashed with an equal amount of potatoes. If you love garlic, beat in some baked garlic purée (see page 136) as well.

Foil-roasted roots have a gloriously intense and deep taste. My advice is to bake batches of the foil-roasted roots every once in a while, and to keep them in the refrigerator to use during the week. It makes as much good sense as keeping cooked rice, canned beans and frozen tomato sauce on hand. With a little pre-planning, sustaining, nutritious, comforting meals are so much easier to throw together at the end of a busy day.

root vegetables: rutabagas, turnips,
celery root, carrots or parsnips

1 Preheat the oven to 425°F.

2 Peel the root vegetables you have chosen. Small roots such as turnips, carrots and small parsnips may be left whole; large ones, such as large parsnips, rutabagas and celery root, should be cut into quarters. Wrap two or three single vegetables or two vegetable quarters loosely in foil, shiny-side in. Crimp well, so that you have a tightly sealed but roomy pouch. Repeat for the remaining vegetables. Bake in the oven for 1-1 1/4 hours or until the vegetables are very tender and beginning to caramelize around the edges.

Gratins of Foil-Roasted Roots

Purées of foil-roasted roots can be put together in all sorts of ways, with all sorts of seasonings. Several examples follow. They are hard to improve upon at the center of a meal, flanked by contrasting accompaniments. Mushroom Ragout (see page 167) and Stir-Fried Peppers (see page 151) go especially well with these gratins.

Simple Gratin of Foil-Roasted Vegetables

· · · · · · · · · · · · · **Z** · · · · · · · · · · · ·

Serves 4

5 foil-roasted white turnips
  (see page 140)
6 foil-roasted medium carrots
  (see page 140)
purée from one head of roasted
  garlic (see page 136)

2-3 tablespoons buttermilk or
  cottage cheese
salt and freshly ground pepper
4 tablespoons grated Parmesan
  cheese

1 Preheat the oven to 350°F (unless preparing ahead of time, see step 3).

2 Purée the vegetables in a blender or food processor until smooth. Add the buttermilk and purée again until well blended. Season with salt and pepper.

3 Scrape the mixture into a small gratin dish or shallow baking dish. Smooth the top and sprinkle with the Parmesan. (The dish may be prepared ahead of time to this point. Refrigerate, well covered, until needed. It will keep for up to two days. Bring to room temperature before proceeding.)

4 Bake, uncovered, in the oven for 30-45 minutes or until browned on top and thoroughly hot. If you wish, to save time, the gratin can be heated in the microwave, then browned under a hot grill.)

Gratin of Baked Potatoes, Onions and Garlic

· · · · · · · · · · · · **Z** · · · · · · · · · · · ·

Serves 4

My favorite gratin combines baked potatoes, onions and garlic. Sweetly earthy, it glorifies mashed potatoes.

4 baking potatoes, baked and
   mashed (see page 173)
purée from 1 head of roasted garlic
   (see page 136)
2 mild onions, baked and puréed
   (see page 138)

4 tablespoons grated Parmesan
   cheese
salt and freshly ground pepper
2-3 tablespoons buttermilk
skim milk

1 Preheat the oven to 350°F (unless preparing ahead of time, see step 3).

2 Put the potato, garlic, onion and cheese in a bowl. Season with salt and pepper, and beat with a wooden spoon. Beat in the buttermilk.

3 Scrape the mixture into a gratin dish and smooth the surface. (The recipe may be prepared in advance to this stage and refrigerated, covered, until needed. Bring to room temperature before proceeding.) Dribble a little skim milk evenly over the top of the vegetables. Bake, uncovered, in the oven for 30-40 minutes or until brown, bubbly and thoroughly hot. (If you wish, to save time, heat through in the microwave, then brown under a hot grill.)

Curried Gratin of Foil-Roasted Vegetables

· · · · · · · · · · · · **Z** · · · · · · · · · · · · ·

Serves 4

A curry infusion (below), or an infusion of Italian seasonings (following recipe), changes the character of roasted vegetable gratins. As you learn the versatility of this technique, you will he able to improvise many different versions.

1 onion, chopped
1/2 teaspoon each of ground
   coriander, ground cumin, mild
   chili powder, paprika and
   ground ginger
salt and freshly ground pepper
1/4 teaspoon ground turmeric
1/4 teaspoon ground allspice
pinch of cayenne
   (or to taste)
1 cup vegetable stock
2 foil-roasted small white turnips,
   puréed or mashed
   (see page 140)

purée from 1 head of foil-roasted
   garlic (see page 136)
2 foil-roasted carrots, puréed
   or mashed (see page 140)
3 foil-roasted small parsnips, puréed
   or mashed (see page 140)
1/2 foil-roasted small rutabaga,
   puréed or mashed (see page 140)
2-3 tablespoons buttermilk
2-3 tablespoons skim milk

1 Preheat the oven to 400°F.

2 Put the onion, spices and stock in a heavy-bottomed frying pan. Cover, bring to boil, and boil for 5-7 minutes. Uncover, reduce heat, and simmer until the onions are tender and the liquid almost gone.

3 Combine the onion and spice mixture with all the puréed vegetables. (To purée the vegetables, cut them into chunks and purée in a blender or food processor until very smooth. Alternatively, mash with a potato masher.) Beat in the buttermilk, then spread the mixture in a gratin dish.

4 Pour a thin drizzle of milk evenly over the top and bake for 30-45 minutes or until bubbly, puffy and browned. (If you wish, to save time, heat through in the microwave, and brown under a hot grill.)

Italian Root Vegetable Gratin

· · · · · · · · · · · · · **❷** · · · · · · · · · · · · ·

Serves 4

The tried and tested sun-dried tomato-scallion infusion is used without garlic in this gratin, because roasted garlic purée is added to the vegetable mixture. Rutabagas and turnips are not particularly Italian, but the infusion bestows upon them an honorary Italian aura.

2-3 dry-packed sun-dried
  tomatoes, coarsely chopped
  (use scissors)
pinch of crushed dried chilies
pinch of dried oregano
6 scallions, sliced
1 cup vegetable stock
6 foil-roasted carrots
  (see page 140)
3 foil-roasted small white turnips
  (see page 140)

1/2 foil-roasted small rutabaga
  (see page 140)
purée from 1 head of foil-roasted
  garlic (see page 136)
3 tablespoons cottage cheese
salt and freshly ground pepper
2 tablespoons grated Parmesan
  cheese
a few tablespoons of skimmed
  milk

1 Preheat the oven to 425°F.

2 Put the sun-dried tomatoes, chilies, oregano, scallions and stock in a heavy-bottomed frying pan. Cover and boil for 5-7 minutes. Uncover, reduce the heat, and simmer until the onion is tender and the liquid almost gone. Leave to cool slightly.

3 Put this infusion in a food processor or blender with the foil-roasted vegetables, garlic and cottage cheese, and process to a purée. Season with salt and pepper.

4 Spread the mixture in a gratin dish. Sprinkle with Parmesan cheese and pour a thin drizzle of milk evenly over the top of the gratin.

5 Bake in the oven for 30-45 minutes or until bubbly, puffy and browned on top. (To save time, heat through in the microwave, and then brown under a hot grill.)

Oven-Braised Vegetables

Oven-braising in stock in an open baking dish is another fat-free method of making the most of various vegetables' natural goodness. Three examples follow, but you could also apply the method to thickly sliced (or quartered) zucchini; peeled and quartered kohlrabi; and cauliflower florets.

Oven-Braised Fennel

. . . .

Serves 4

Fennel looks like bulbous celery and tastes of anise. There is a scene in the film Star Wars, *when Luke Skywalker's Aunt Beru prepares a meal by putting bulbs of fennel into a sort of other-worldly food processor. I suppose director George Lucas thought that a vegetable resembling alien celery was just right for extraterrestrial home cooking!*

2 fennel bulbs, cut in half
   lengthwise
1/2 cup vegetable stock

salt and freshly ground pepper
3 tablespoons grated Parmesan
   cheese

1 Preheat the oven to 350°F.

2 Cut each fennel half into wedges about 1/2-inch wide. Arrange the fennel in one layer in a baking dish. Pour over the stock and season with salt and pepper.

3 Bake, uncovered, in the oven for 45 minutes, sprinkling the Parmesan over the fennel for the last 15 minutes. The fennel will become meltingly tender and the stock will have cooked almost completely away, leaving a rich glaze. Serve at once.

Ⓥ Omit the Parmesan cheese.

Oven-Braised Eggplant, Chinese-Style

· · · · · · · · · · · **Ⓥ** · · · · · · · · · · · ·

Makes 4 cups—Serves 4

Eggplant's sponge-like character is perfect for oven-braising—it soaks up the Chinese flavorings most deliciously.

6 small eggplants, cut into
   1-inch cubes
3 garlic cloves, crushed
1/2-inch piece of fresh ginger,
   peeled and crushed

1 tablespoon teriyaki sauce
3 tablespoons medium dry
   sherry
1 cup vegetable stock
freshly ground pepper

1 Preheat the oven to 350°F.

2 Spread the eggplant in a shallow baking or gratin dish. Mix the remaining ingredients together and pour over the eggplant. Bake, uncovered, in the oven for 45 minutes to 1 hour or until the eggplant is tender and deeply delicious, shaking the pan and stirring up the vegetable pieces occasionally. Serve hot.

Oven-Braised Jerusalem Artichokes

· · · · · · · · · · · **V** · · · · · · · · · · · ·

Jerusalem artichokes are rough, knobby roots that are neither artichokes, nor from Jerusalem, although their flavor does bear some resemblance to that of French globe artichokes. Their texture is pleasurably starchy, although one of the starches they contain is inulin, which makes some people very "windy"—others don't seem bothered at all. You don't know until you try them—and they really are very good to eat.

olive oil and water spray
  (see page 5)
vegetable stock

Jerusalem artichokes, peeled
  and halved
freshly ground pepper (optional)

1 Preheat the oven to 200°C.

2 Mist a baking dish with olive oil spray, and pour in a few tablespoons of stock. Put the artichokes in, cut-sides down, and roast in the oven for 35-45 minutes or until they are tender, browned and sizzling, stirring occasionally. If necessary, add a few more drops of stock now and then, but don't swamp the artichokes.

3 Season with pepper, if desired, and serve.

Stir-Frying in Stock

Stir-frying usually depends on oil, but it can easily be done with stock, either in a wok or in a large frying pan. Some vegetables (zucchini and peppers, for example) can just be tossed around in stock (and whatever seasoning you like) until they are tender and the liquid has cooked down. Others (cauliflower and broccoli, for example) need a combination of stir-frying and simmering to reach tenderness. It is an option to steam the vegetable to partial tenderness first, and then quickly to stir-fry in a flavorful infusion to finish it off. Several recipes follow, to get you started.

Stir-Fried Zucchini

· · · · · · · · · · · **Ⓥ** · · **Ⓩ** · · · · · · · · · · · ·

Serves 2–4

6 small zucchini
1/2 cup vegetable stock
salt and freshly ground pepper

generous pinch of ground cumin
juice of 1 lime

1 Wash and trim the zucchini but do not peel them. Cut them in half and then into strips about 2 inches long and 1/2-inch wide.

2 Pour the stock into a heavy-bottomed frying pan or wok, and bring to a boil. Throw in the zucchini, grind in a generous amount of pepper, and sprinkle in the cumin. With two wooden spoons, constantly toss and turn the vegetables over high heat until they are crisp-tender, and the stock has cooked down to almost nothing. Squeeze in the lime juice, season lightly with salt and let the zucchini stir-fry for a minute or so in their own juices.

VARIATIONS

Stir-Fried Zucchini with Garlic and Ginger

Crush a clove of garlic and a thin slice of peeled ginger. Put them in a frying pan with the stock and 1-2 tablespoons dry sherry, and boil for a few seconds before throwing in the zucchini. Omit the pepper and the lime juice. Sprinkle with some chopped fresh cilantro before serving.

Italian Sweet and Sour Zucchini

Add two cloves of crushed garlic to the stock and boil for a few seconds. Throw in the zucchini, freshly ground pepper, 2 tablespoons each of raisins, capers (drained and rinsed), and the juice of 1 lemon. Just before serving, stir in some finely chopped parsley. Serve hot or cold.

Stir-Fried Cauliflower

· · · · · · · · · · **Ⓥ** · · **Ⓩ** · · · · · · · · · · · ·

Serves 2–4

In this stir-fry, cauliflower is given the full non-fat Italian treatment. Because cauliflower is such a good flavor absorber, it takes deliciously to this treatment.

1 cup vegetable stock
4 scallions, sliced
pinch of crushed dried chilies
  (optional)
1 garlic clove, crushed
2 black olives in brine, drained
  drained and flesh slivered
  off the stones

2 dry-packed sun-dried tomatoes,
  chopped (use scissors)
1 large cauliflower, separated
  into florets
salt and freshly ground pepper

1 Put 3/4 cup of the stock, scallions, chilies, garlic, olive pieces and sun-dried tomatoes in a wide heavy-bottomed frying pan or wok. Boil for 4-5 minutes. Toss in the cauliflower, and season with salt and pepper. Add the remaining stock, cover and simmer for 3 minutes.

2 Uncover the pan and turn the heat to high. Stir and toss the florets in the boiling stock until the stock is almost gone and the cauliflower is crisp-tender.

Stir-Fried Peppers

· · · · · · · · · · · **V** · · **Z** · · · · · · · · · · · ·

Makes 1 1/2 cups

Peppers take to stock stir-frying remarkably well. The juices cook down to a buttery sauce-like consistency and the pepper pieces become supple and lusciously tender. Stir-fried peppers make an excellent side dish, as well as a colorful garnish for many other dishes. The technique only works if the peppers have been peeled.

4-6 red or yellow peppers   freshly ground pepper
3/4-1 cup vegetable stock

1 Cut the peppers lengthwise in half. Remove the stems, the seeds and the ribs, and cut the halves into their natural sections. Peel each piece with a swivel-bladed vegetable peeler, then cut into strips about 1/2-inch wide.

2 Heat the stock in a heavy-bottomed frying pan. When very hot, toss in the peppers and grind in some black pepper. Stir and turn the peppers in the hot stock until the liquid has cooked down considerably. Turn down the heat a little and fry the peppers in their own juices for a few minutes or until they are very tender, and the pepper juices have formed a thick sauce. Serve at once, with their delicious juices, or serve at room temperature. This dish may be made in advance and rewarmed later or on the next day.

Cauliflower and Peppers

Ⓥ · · Ⓩ

Serves 4

Cauliflower and peppers make a stunning pair. For a change, substitute fennel or anise seeds for the cumin.

I large cauliflower, separated into
 florets
2 large red peppers, deseeded
 and cut lengthwise into their
 natural sections

3/4 cup vegetable stock
I garlic clove, crushed
1/2 teaspoon cumin seeds
salt and freshly ground pepper

1 Steam the cauliflower florets over boiling water for about 5 minutes or until partially cooked. Refresh under cold running water and set aside.

2 With a swivel-bladed vegetable peeler, peel each pepper piece. Cut the peppers into strips about 1/2-inch wide.

3 Heat half the stock in a heavy-bottomed frying pan. When it begins to bubble, stir in the garlic and peppers. Stir and toss with two wooden spoons until the peppers are almost tender and the liquid almost gone. Lower the heat and let the peppers fry gently in their own juices as you stir them. When they are tender, stir in the cauliflower.

4 Sprinkle in the cumin and stir well. Pour in the remaining stock, stir and cook until the cauliflower is tender but not mushy. Season with salt and pepper.

Peperonata

· · · · · · · · · · · · · **V** · · **Z** · · · · · · · · · · · · ·

Serves 4—Makes 2 1/2 cups

The addition of onion, vermouth, olives and capers turns stir-fried peppers into a vibrant Italian side dish.

6 large red peppers
I large mild onion
2 garlic cloves, crushed
2 black olives in brine, drained
    and flesh slivered off the stones
1/4 cup dry white vermouth

3/4 cup vegetable stock
I tablespoon drained capers
salt and freshly ground pepper
2 tablespoons chopped fresh
   parsley

1 Cut the peppers lengthwise in half. Remove the stems, the seeds and the ribs, and cut the halves into their natural sections. Peel with a swivel-bladed vegetable peeler, and cut each piece into strips about 1/2-inch wide. Cut the onion in half, and then cut each half into thin halfmoons.

2 Put the peppers, onion, garlic, olives, vermouth, stock and capers in a heavy-bottomed frying pan. Grind in some pepper and bring to a boil, then reduce the heat and cook the vegetables, tossing and turning them in the stock until the liquid has cooked down considerably.

3 Let the vegetables fry in their own juices until beautifully tender. Salt lightly, if necessary, and stir in the parsley. Serve hot or cold as a salad, a relish, a sandwich filling or a vegetable.

Stir-Fried Asparagus

· · · · · · · · · · · · **Ⓥ** · · · · · · · · · · · · ·

The best way to treat asparagus is to prepare the stalks as in step 1, below, then to steam them over boiling water for 3-7 minutes only (depending on their size) until they just bend a little when lifted with tongs. Blot dry with paper towels, and serve with Yellow Pepper Sauce (see page 100). Pick up each stalk with your fingers, dabble in the sauce, and eat. The stir-frying method described below is the next best method. During the asparagus season, alternate the methods (or have one for lunch, one for dinner, if you are as much of an asparagus fanatic as I am).

fresh, thick asparagus	pinch of dried thyme
1/2 cup vegetable stock	pinch of dried tarragon
1/2 lime	salt and freshly ground pepper

1 Cut off the tough, woody, bottom portion of each asparagus stalk. With a swivel-bladed vegetable peeler, peel each stalk from the bottom up to the tip. If you are not going to cook the stalks at once, stand them in a glass of water as if they were a bunch of flowers.

2 Cut the asparagus into 1-inch lengths. Heat the stock in a non-reactive wok or frying pan. Throw in the asparagus and toss and turn in the hot stock for about 2 minutes (use two wooden spoons or spatulas).

3 Squeeze in the juice of 1/2 lime, add a pinch each of thyme and tarragon, and season with salt and pepper. Continue to stir-fry for a few moments more or until the asparagus is crisp-tender (more crisp than tender). Serve at once.

Glazed Turnips

· · · · · · · · · · · · **V** · · · · · · · · · · · · ·

Serves 4

Both turnips and carrot benefit from stir-frying in a mixture of stock, citrus juice and complementary seasonings. The turnips are boiled in this flavorful mixture first, then simmered and stirred until tender and glazed; the carrots (below) are simply stir-fried.

1 1/2 lbs small white turnips, peeled and cut into 1/2-inch wedges	1/4 cup fresh orange juice
	1 tablespoon hoisin sauce
	1 teaspoon sugar
1 cup vegetable stock	salt and freshly ground pepper

1 Put all the ingredients in a frying pan that can be covered. Cover, bring to a boil, and boil for 7-8 minutes.

2 Uncover, reduce the heat, and simmer, stirring occasionally, until the turnips are meltingly tender and bathed in a syrupy glaze.

Spiced Carrots

· · · · · · · · · · **V** · · **Z** · · · · · · · · · · ·

Makes 2 cups—Serves 2–4

2 cups vegetable stock	1/2 teaspoon sugar
4 garlic cloves, crushed	juice of 1 small lemon
1/2 teaspoon ground cumin	1 lb carrots, sliced
pinch of ground cinnamon	salt and freshly ground pepper
pinch of cayenne	

1 Put all the ingredients except the carrots, salt and pepper in a heavy bottomed saucepan. Cover and boil for 3-4 minutes.

2 Uncover, stir in the carrots and season with salt and pepper. Cook, uncovered, stirring and tossing, until the carrots are tender, and the liquid has cooked down to a syrupy glaze.

Curries and Stews

Go vegetable mad! Sweep down the fresh produce aisles and gather up armfuls of the best-looking roots, bulbs, shoots, greens, reds and yellows. Bring the vegetable treasure home for peeling, dicing and slicing, then toss them into infusions of herbs and spices and cook until they soak up all the spicy flavor, yet their own vegetable goodness shines through. Serve heaped platters of these steamy, fragrant stews and curries with rice or other grains, along with a chutney or salsa or two, and cottage cheese mixed with a few chopped herbs.

SERVING NOTE

Serving size depends on appetite, and how many other dishes will be served with the stew. For a main dish mixed-vegetable curry or stew, 1 1/2-2 cups equals one serving; for a single vegetable curry, like Curried Cabbage (below) and Mushroom Ragout (see page 167), about 1 cup equals one serving because they are best served as part of a selection of vegetable dishes. These are very general rules.

Curried Cabbage

. . . .

Makes 2 cups

The important thing when preparing fat-free curries is to ensure that the onions and curry spices cook gently in stock long enough for the spices to lose their harsh, raw character. It only takes 10-12 minutes altogether, but they are important minutes.

1 large onion, halved and cut into thin halfmoons	1/2 teaspoon ground coriander
2 garlic cloves, crushed	2 cups vegetable stock
1/4 teaspoon each mild chili powder, ground cinnamon, ground turmeric and ground ginger	1 small white cabbage, cored, trimmed of tough outer leaves, quartered and shredded (use a sharp kitchen knife, or the processor)
pinch of ground allspice	1/4-1/2 lime
1 teaspoon paprika	salt and freshly ground pepper
1 teaspoon ground cumin	

I Put the onion, garlic, spices and 1 cup stock in a heavy-bottomed frying pan. Cover and boil for 5-7 minutes. Reduce the heat a little and simmer, stirring frequently, until the vegetables and spices are frying in their own juices.

2 Stir in the cabbage and remaining stock. Simmer, uncovered, for 15-20 minutes or until the cabbage is tender and the sauce is thick and savory. Squeeze in a little lime juice, taste and adjust the seasonings.

Curried Cauliflower

· · · · · · · · · · **V** · · **Z** · · · · · · · · · ·

Makes 2 cups

Potatoes and cauliflower are able to soak up beautiful spice infusions without losing their own character. In this recipe, the cauliflower soaks alone; in the following recipe, it pairs up with its rival.

I mild onion, chopped
3 garlic cloves, crushed
1/2 teaspoon ground turmeric
2 teaspoons ground coriander
I teaspoon ground cumin
I teaspoon garam masala
1/4 teaspoon cayenne

I cup vegetable stock
I 14-oz can of chopped
   tomatoes
I large cauliflower, separated into
   florets
salt and freshly ground pepper

I Put the onion, garlic, spices and stock in a heavy-bottomed frying pan. Cover and boil for 5-7 minutes. Uncover, reduce the heat a little, and simmer, stirring frequently, until the onions and spices are frying in their own juices.

2 Stir in the tomatoes and the cauliflower, and season with salt and pepper. Cover and simmer for 15 minutes. Uncover and simmer, stirring occasionally, for an additional 15-20 minutes or until the cauliflower is tender and the sauce thick and savory.

Potato and Cauliflower Curry

· · · · · · · · · · · Ⓥ · · Ⓩ · · · · · · · · · · · ·

Makes 6 cups

Serve this with the usual: rice, raita, a chutney (or two or three), and finish with something indulgently fruity—a mango, or a handful of fresh lychees.

3 large onions, each cut into
    8 wedges
1/2-inch piece of ginger,
    peeled and crushed
2 garlic cloves, crushed
1/2 teaspoon ground turmeric
1/4 teaspoon cayenne
1 1/2 teaspoons ground coriander
1/2 teaspoon ground cardamom
1/2 teaspoon ground allspice

2 cups vegetable stock
1 tablespoon tomato purée
1 medium cauliflower, separated
    into florets
3 medium potatoes, scrubbed and
    cut into 1/2-inch cubes
salt and freshly ground pepper
chopped fresh cilantro, to garnish

1 Put the onions, ginger, garlic, spices and 1 cup stock in a heavy-bottomed frying pan. Cover and boil for 5-7 minutes. Uncover, reduce the heat, and simmer, stirring occasionally, until the onions and spices are frying in their own juices. Stir in the tomato purée.

2 Purée half the mixture in a blender or food processor, and return it to the pan.

3 Stir in the cauliflower, potato and remaining stock. Cover and simmer, stirring occasionally, until the vegetables are tender and the sauce is thick and savory. Season with salt and pepper, and serve garnished with cilantro.

Vegetable Curry

· · · · · · · · · · · **V** · · **Z** · · · · · · · · · · · ·

Makes 6 cups

The next three recipes for mixed vegetable curries take full advantage of our modern vegetable bounty and the non-fat onion-spice sauté method. This mixture features fennel, cauliflower and zucchini.

I large mild onion, coarsely
   chopped
2-4 garlic cloves, crushed
I 1/2 teaspoons ground cumin
I 1/2 teaspoons ground coriander
1/4 teaspoon ground allspice
1/4 teaspoon cayenne
1/2 teaspoon ground ginger
I teaspoon ground turmeric
I teaspoon paprika
3 cups vegetable stock
3 celery stalks, cut into 1/2-inch
   slices
3 carrots, coarsely chopped
3 small white turnips, peeled and
   coarsely chopped

3 peppers (I red, I green, I yellow),
   peeled, deseeded and coarsely
   chopped
I fennel bulb, cut into 1/2-inch slices
I lb zucchini, cut into 1/2-inch slices
small cauliflower, separated into
   florets
juice of I medium lemon
salt and freshly ground pepper
6 tablespoons chopped fresh
   parsley
4 tablespoons chopped fresh
   cilantro

I Put the onion, garlic, spices and 1 cup stock in a heavy-bottomed frying pan. Cover, bring to a boil, and boil for 5-7 minutes. Stir in the celery, carrots, turnips, peppers and fennel, reduce the heat a little, and simmer, stirring frequently, until the vegetables and spices are frying in their own juices.

2 Stir in the remaining ingredients, except the herbs, but including the remaining 2 cups stock. Season with salt and pepper, and simmer gently, covered, for 20-25 minutes or until all the vegetables are tender. Stir in the herbs just before serving.

Vegetable Curry
in Vegetable Sauce

· · · · · · · · · · · · **Z** · · · · · · · · · · · ·

Makes 8 cups

The rich sauce for this curry is produced by puréeing some of the spice-infused vegetables—very simple to do with a blender or food processor.

2 large mild onions, each cut into
   8 pieces
2 garlic cloves, crushed
1 tablespoon each of ground
   cumin, ground coriander
   and paprika
1/2 teaspoon each of ground
   allspice, ground cardamom
   and ground ginger
1 teaspoon ground turmeric
1/4 teaspoon cayenne
   (or to taste)
about 2 cups vegetable stock
3 medium peppers, peeled,
   deseeded and coarsely chopped
3 large carrots, coarsely chopped
3/4 lb button mushrooms,
   halved or quartered

medium white turnips, cut into
   1/2-inch pieces
1 large cauliflower, separated into
   florets
1 small parsnip, cut into 1/2-inch
   pieces
1 fennel bulb, quartered and cut into
   1/2-inch slices
3 celery stalks, cut into 1/2-inch
   slices
salt
juice of 1/2 large lemon
3 medium zucchini, cut into
   1/2-inch slices
1/2 lb string beans, cut into
   1/2-inch pieces
Mint and Cilantro Raita (see page
   191) or Creamy Herb Sauce
   (see page 192), to garnish

1 Put the onion pieces, garlic, spices and 1 cup stock in a heavy-bottomed saucepan. Cover and boil for 5-7 minutes. Uncover and stir in the peppers, carrots and mushrooms. Reduce the heat slightly and simmer, stirring frequently, until the vegetables and spices are frying in their own juices, and the vegetables are tender. Leave to cool slightly.

2 Purée half the mixture in a blender or food processor, then return the purée to the pan.

3 Add the turnip, cauliflower, parsnip, fennel and celery. Stir together very well. Add enough stock almost to cover the contents of the pot, season with salt, and bring to a boil.

4 Reduce the heat, cover, and simmer for 15 minutes. Uncover, squeeze in the lemon juice, and add the zucchini and beans. Simmer uncovered for 10 minutes more, or until all the vegetables are tender. Serve in deep soup bowls, each serving garnished with a dollop of Raita or Creamy Herb Sauce.

V Omit the Raita or Creamy Herb Sauce.

Vegetable Curry with Corn Cobs

· · · · · · · · · · · · **2** · · · · · · · · · · · ·

Makes 7 cups

Adorable dwarf corn cobs (which can be eaten whole) star in this curry, along with co-stars fennel and mushrooms, and the usual carrots and celery. Parsnips and turnips make their appearance, too. You could eat a vegetable curry or chili every night for a year and never repeat yourself and never grow bored—at least I could!

2 mild onions, coarsely chopped
4 garlic cloves, crushed
1 teaspoon mild chili powder
1 teaspoon dried oregano
1 tablespoon paprika
1 tablespoon ground cilantro
1/2 teaspoon ground cinnamon
1/4 teaspoon ground allspice
pinch of ground cloves
2 teaspoons ground cumin
1 1/2 cups vegetable stock
3 celery stalks, cut into
    1/2-inch slices
3 carrots, coarsely chopped
1 fennel bulb, quartered and
    cut into 1/2-inch slices
1/2 lb button mushrooms,
    halved or quartered

3 peppers (1 red, 1 yellow, 1 green),
    peeled, deseeded and coarsely
    chopped, or use canned
    peppers
2 14-oz cans of chopped
    tomatoes
2 medium white turnips, chopped
    into 1/2-inch cubes
1 small parsnip, chopped into
    1/2-inch cubes
salt and freshly ground pepper
8 dwarf corn cobs, sliced
    into 1-inch pieces
1/2 lb string beans, cut into
    1-inch pieces
Mint and Cilantro Raita (see
    page 191) and thinly sliced
    scallions, to garnish

1 Put the onion pieces, garlic, spices and 1 cup stock in a heavy-bottomed saucepan. Cover and boil for 5-7 minutes. Uncover and stir in the celery, carrots, fennel, mushrooms, peppers and a bit more stock. Simmer, stirring occasionally, until the vegetables and spices are frying in their own juices. Cook gently for a few more minutes, stirring.

2 Stir in the tomatoes, turnip and parsnip. Season with salt and pepper, and simmer for 10 minutes.

3 Stir in the corn cobs and runner beans. Simmer for about another 10 minutes or until all the vegetables are tender. Serve in soup bowls, each garnished with a dollop of Raita and a sprinkling of scallions.

Ⓥ Omit the Raita.

Vegetable Chili with Potatoes

· · · · · · · · · · · · **Z** · · · · · · · · · · · ·

Makes 7 cups

Mexican food is a complex and interesting cuisine based on spice pastes, chilies and ground seeds and nuts—in some ways reminiscent of the cuisines of parts of India. Like Indian cuisine (indeed like most of the world's cuisines), it is fat-based, but again like most cuisines, it adapts well to low-fat techniques.

I mild onion, coarsely chopped
2-4 garlic cloves, crushed
3 celery stalks, cut into
　1/2-inch slices
3 carrots, coarsely chopped
I tablespoon each of paprika,
　mild chili powder and
　ground cumin
1/2 tablespoon ground cilantro
1/4 teaspoon ground cinnamon
I teaspoon dried oregano
I cup vegetable stock

3 peppers (I red, I yellow, I green),
　peeled, deseeded and coarsely
　chopped
2 14-oz cans of chopped
　tomatoes
2 potatoes, cut into I-inch cubes
4 small zucchini, cut into
　1/2-inch slices
I large cauliflower, separated into
　florets
salt and freshly ground pepper
cottage cheese and chopped fresh
　cilantro, to garnish

1 Put the onion, garlic, celery, carrots, spices, oregano and 1 cup stock in a heavy-bottomed frying pan. Cover and boil for 5-7 minutes. Uncover, stir in the peppers, and simmer, stirring frequently, until the vegetables and spices are frying in their own juices.

2 Stir in the tomatoes and potatoes. Simmer for 5 minutes, then stir in the zucchini and cauliflower. Season with salt and pepper, and add a little more stock, if necessary. Simmer for 20-25 minutes or until the mixture is thick and the cauliflower and potatoes are tender. Serve with small bowls of the garnishes.

V Omit the cottage cheese garnish.

Lesco-Potato Stew

· · · · · · · · · · · · **❷** · · · · · · · · · · · ·

Makes 6 cups

Lesco is a Hungarian mélange of onions, peppers and paprika (plus lard or goose fat, but let's not dwell on that). Hungarians seem to cook lesco with everything, which is not a bad thing—it is delicious. Lesco goes particularly well with potatoes (but then, most things go particularly well with potatoes).

3 large mild onions, coarsely
   chopped
2 garlic cloves, crushed
2 tablespoons paprika
1 teaspoon dried marjoram
about 1 1/2 cups vegetable stock
3 large peppers (1 red, 1 green,
   1 yellow), peeled, deseeded and
   coarsely chopped
salt and freshly ground pepper

1-2 pinches of cayenne
   (optional)
2 14-oz cans of chopped
   tomatoes
4 medium potatoes, scrubbed and
   cut into 1-inch cubes
cottage cheese and snipped fresh
   dill to garnish

1 Put the onions, garlic, paprika, marjoram and 1 cup stock in a heavy-bottomed saucepan. Cover and boil for 5-7 minutes. Uncover and stir in the peppers. Simmer for a few minutes more until the mixture is very thick, the vegetables and paprika are frying in their own juices, and the liquid is almost gone.

2 Stir in the remaining ingredients (except the cottage cheese and dill), and add enough stock barely to cover the contents of the pan. Bring to a boil, then reduce the heat, cover and simmer for 20-30 minutes or until the potatoes are tender. Serve in soup bowls garnished with a dollop of cottage cheese and a sprinkling of snipped fresh dill.

Ⓥ Omit the cottage cheese garnish.

Turnip and Potato Stew

· · · · · · · · · · · **V** · · **Z** · · · · · · · · · · ·

Makes 5 cups

Little white turnips have a delicately peppery flavor. They are lovely raw, as part of a crudité selection, but they also marry well with potatoes in a vegetable stew.

2 medium onions, halved and sliced into paper-thin halfmoons
3 garlic cloves, crushed
3/4 cup vegetable stock
3 small peppers (1 red, 1 yellow, 1 green), peeled, deseeded and sliced
3 small white turnips, coarsely diced

1 14-oz can of tomatoes, drained and cut into strips
salt and freshly ground pepper
3 small potatoes, coarsely diced
3 tablespoons chopped fresh parsley

1 Put the onions, garlic and stock in a frying pan. Cover and boil for 3-4 minutes.

2 Uncover, reduce the heat slightly, and simmer briskly, stirring, until the onions are tender. Stir in the peppers and cook for a few minutes until they soften.

3 Stir in the turnips and tomatoes, and season with salt and pepper. Cover and simmer very gently for 10 minutes. Add the potatoes, recover and simmer until the turnips, potatoes and peppers are tender. Stir in the parsley.

Mushroom Ragout

· · · · · · · · · · **Ⓥ** · · **Ⓩ** · · · · · · · · · ·

Makes 3 cups

The reconstituted dried mushrooms give this ragout resounding woodsy depths, but it is very good (if less intense) without them, too. The ragout fills a rice crust (see page 56) nicely, or a boiled or baked potato, or a depression in a mound of mashed potatoes. And it is the perfect partner for one of the foil-roasted vegetable gratins.

3-4 dried shiitake mushrooms
1/2 oz dried *porcini*
   mushrooms
2 lbs mixed fresh mushrooms
   (white and brown caps), cut
   into quarters or eighths
6 scallions, sliced

1/2 teaspoon dried tarragon,
   crumbled
1/4 cup dry sherry
several dashes teriyaki sauce
I heaped tablespoon Dijon
   mustard
freshly ground pepper

I Rinse the dried mushrooms under cold running water, then put them in a bowl and cover with plenty of hot water. Leave to soak for 20 minutes.

2 Tip the dried mushrooms and soaking water through a sieve lined with a double thickness of muslin or coffee filter papers set over a bowl. Reserve mushrooms and soaking liquid.

3 Rinse the soaked mushrooms under cold running water, chop them coarsely (discarding the tough shiitake stems), and put them in a frying pan with the fresh mushrooms. Add 1/2 cup of the soaking liquid, the onions, tarragon, sherry and teriyaki sauce. Cook, stirring occasionally, until the fresh mushrooms have exuded a great deal of liquid.

4 Stir in the mustard, and season with pepper. Simmer until the mushrooms are tender and the liquid greatly reduced.

VARIATION
Creamy Mushroom Ragout

Stir a few spoonfuls of the mushroom soaking liquid or stock into 8 oz ricotta cheese at room temperature. Fold this "cream" into the Mushroom Ragout. Adjust the seasonings.

Roasted Root Vegetable Stew

· · · · · · · · · · **(V)** · · **(Z)** · · · · · · · · · · ·

Makes 5 cups

A combination of roots, bulbs and stalks is roasted in an open pan and then enriched with a mustard, sherry and tarragon sauce. Peel and cube the sweet potato at the last minute; it turns dark if it sits around.

Olive oil and water spray
  (see page 5)
I head of garlic, cloves separated
  and peeled
I mild onion, halved and cut into
  1/2-inch wedges
I fennel bulb, halved and cut into
  1/2-inch slices
I small (or 1/2 large) rutabaga, peeled
  and cut into 1/2-inch pieces
I large parsnip, cut into 1/2-inch
  pieces (if the core is tough
  and woody, cut it away)
2 carrots, cut into 1/2-inch slices

2 celery stalks, cut into
  1/2-inch slices
I medium sweet potato, cut into
  1/2-inch pieces
I cup vegetable stock
2-3 tablespoons medium dry
  sherry
1/2 teaspoon dried tarragon,
  crumbled
I tablespoon Dijon mustard
2 tablespoons tomato purée
3-4 dashes of teriyaki or soy sauce
juice of 1/2 large lemon
salt and freshly ground pepper

1 Preheat the oven to 450°F.

2 Lightly mist a wide, shallow baking dish with the oil spray. Spread all the vegetables in the dish and mist the vegetables lightly with the spray. Pour in 1/2 cup stock, and stir to combine everything. Bake, uncovered, in the oven for 30 minutes, stirring once or twice.

3 Pour the sherry into the dish, and stir and scrape with a wooden spoon to dislodge the browned bits on the bottom of the dish. Reduce the oven temperature to 350°F.

4 In a measuring cup, mix the remaining stock with the tarragon, mustard, tomato purée, teriyaki or soy sauce and lemon juice. Stir into the stew and season with salt and pepper. Bake for a further 10-15 minutes.

Cauliflower Paprikash

. . . .

Makes 3 cups

Hungarian cuisine is one of the most interesting in the world, but the frequent appearance of lard or goose fat and sour cream make it one of the fattiest as well. The use of paprika (the ground dried pods of the red capsicum pepper) make the cuisine distinctive; the rosy blush of a paprika-sour cream sauce is a characteristic of many Hungarian dishes. In the first step of a Hungarian sauce, paprika, like curry spices, is always gently cooked in butter, lard or oil with the flavoring vegetables. Cook it gently in stock instead. Ricotta cheese stands in for cream, giving a delicious creaminess for a fraction of the fat content.

I large mild onion, chopped
I garlic clove, crushed
1/2 teaspoon dried marjoram,
    crumbled (optional)
2 carrots, chopped
2 red peppers, peeled,
    deseeded and chopped
2-3 dry-packed sun-dried
    tomatoes, chopped

I tablespoon paprika
2 1/2 cups vegetable stock
1/2 cup dry vermouth
I cauliflower, separated into
    florets
I cup tomato purée
salt and freshly ground pepper
I 1/2 oz ricotta cheese

I Put the onion, garlic, marjoram (if using), carrots, peppers, sun-dried tomatoes, paprika, 2 cups stock and the vermouth in a flame-proof casserole. Cover and boil for 5-7 minutes. Uncover, reduce the heat, and simmer until the vegetables and paprika are gently frying in their own juices.

2 Stir in the cauliflower, tomato purée and remaining stock. Season with salt and pepper, and simmer, partially covered, for 20-30 minutes or until the cauliflower is very tender, stirring occasionally.

3 Put the ricotta in a blender or food processor with a few spoonfuls of the sauce, and purée. Stir this creamy purée back into the casserole, and bring back to barely simmering. Taste, and adjust seasonings, if necessary.

Potatoes

The potato, that starchy and delicious culinary wonder, is not just another vegetable. With its comforting, substantial and versatile qualities, it can form the basis of a meal like nothing else.

Potatoes originated in the Andes of South America at least 8,000 years ago, and eventually became a significant staple—spiritual, economic and nutritional—of the Inca Empire. It wasn't until the exploration of the so-called New World that potatoes found their way to Europe. Much romantic folklore attributes the momentous introduction of the potato in Europe to Sir Walter Raleigh, or Sir Francis Drake, but it was most likely a nameless, but ethnobotanically curious, Spanish sailor who first brought the potato to European shores. Potatoes are so deeply entrenched in our food habits that it is startling to realize that they have been around only since the sixteenth century. And they weren't exactly welcomed with open arms (or mouths) either. People throughout Europe refused to have anything to do with the strange tubers; they were believed to be evil, decadent, and as poisonous as their relative, deadly nightshade.

Times change. The only fear of potatoes people harbor these days is that spuds will make them fat. Nonsense! A potato contains virtually no fat, pretty good protein, and a nice package of fiber, vitamins and minerals. Treat them right (don't douse them in high-fat ingredients) and potatoes will comfort and sustain you through a lifetime of happy and healthy eating.

Baked Potatoes

· · · · · · · · · · · · **Ⓥ** · · · · · · · · · · · · ·

The best baked potatoes take time, in a hot oven. Preheat the oven to 425°F. Scrub the potatoes, then pierce in several places with a fork or thin skewer. Bake directly on the oven rack for 1 1/4-1 1/2 hours, turning once during baking. When done, the potatoes are creamy-fluffy on the inside and delightfully crunchy on the outside.

Always open your potatoes like this: with a fork, perforate the potato on top in a dotted "X." Then squeeze, so that the fluffy potato flesh surges up through the crunchy skin. If you use a knife to cut them open, instead of perforating with a fork and squeezing, the texture will be slightly lumpy, instead of the glorious fluffy, creamy, steamy texture that—against the crunchiness of the skin—makes a baked potato such a pleasure to eat.

Baked potatoes are delicious with freshly ground pepper, a squeeze of fresh lemon, a dollop of cottage cheese or one of the dips, spreads, sauces or raitas in this book. A perfect, large baked potato, overflowing with your chosen filling, makes a sustaining and delicious main course.

Baked Potato Halves

· · · · · · · · · · · · **V** · · · · · · · · · · · · ·

Baking potatoes in the microwave is fast, but you end up with steamed potatoes, quite different from the real crunchy-skinned, fluffy-fleshed thing. If you combine the microwave and the conventional oven you save quite a bit of time, yet the results are exemplary: potato halves that are as fluffy as mashed potatoes on the inside, as crunchy as chips on the outside. As with all recipes using the oven (both microwave and conventional), use the times as a guide only.

1 Preheat the conventional oven to its highest setting.

Halve two baking potatoes. Put a double sheet of absorbent kitchen paper towels on the microwave turntable. Place the potatoes, skin-side down, on the paper. Microwave on high (100%) for 5 minutes.

2 Turn the potatoes skin-side up, and microwave on high (100%) for another 5 minutes.

3 Place the potatoes directly on the rack of the conventional oven, skin-side down, and bake for 10 minutes. Turn skin-side up and bake for another 10 minutes. When golden, puffed and cooked through, the potatoes are ready. Serve at once. Eat just as they are or serve with a dollop of Roasted Tomato Ketchup (see page 93) or Tomato Sauce (see pages 91-92) and a dollop of Creamy Herb Sauce (see page 192). Dip the potatoes into each of the two dollops, as you eat them.

Mashed Baked Potatoes

· ·

To make exceptional mashed potatoes, bake them first (see page 171). Scoop the baked flesh out of the baked potatoes into a bowl. Mash well with an old-fashioned potato masher or—if you want a fluffier consistancy—push through a ricer. With a wooden spoon, beat in some cottage cheese or buttermilk, and beat in a little grated Parmesan or low-fat cheddar along with salt and freshly ground pepper to taste. Pile the mashed potatoes into a large bowl. Garnish around the edges with whatever takes your fancy: Mushroom Ragout (see page 167), Stir-Fried Peppers (see page 151), spinach. Or make a crater in the potatoes and fill with Green Split Pea Dhal (see page 113), Gravy (see page 94), one of the tomato or pepper sauces, Peperonata (see page 153) or Herbed Eggplant Sauce (see page 96). I'm sure you get the idea.

The advantages of the baked-potato method of making mashed spuds are twofold:

• *The quality of the mash is the best it can be.*

• *You have those seductive potato skins left over, just begging to be eaten. Eat them on the spot, or refrigerate them and save them for an indulgent snack. At snack time, cut them into strips, and grill, inside-up, for a few minutes (not too long) to crisp them. Grind on some pepper and salt lightly, if you wish. Eat plain, or with a dip or sauce. Or make a light meal out of them: cut each whole potato skin into eight pieces, arrange inside-up on a baking sheet, fill each piece with a dab of tomato sauce, top with low-fat mozzarella and grill.*

Thick Potato Chips

· · · · · · · · · · · **Ⓥ** · · · · · · · · · · · ·

With an atomizer oil and water spray (see page 5), a non-stick baking sheet and a hot oven, you can have chips that rival the real, boiled-in-oil thing. How nice to bite into a chip and taste potatoes—not a mouthful of grease! As with all oven recipes, adjust the time to suit your oven.

oil and water spray (see page 5)
baking potatoes

1 Preheat the oven to 425°F.

2 Don't bother to peel the potatoes. Just scrub them and cut them across into 1/4- to 1/2-inch slices. Cut each slice in half.

3 You will need one or two flat non-stick baking sheets. Mist them lightly with the oil spray. Spread the potatoes on the sheet(s) in one layer, put them in the oven and leave them for 20-30 minutes.

4 Pull the potatoes out and gently turn them with a spatula. Return them to the oven for a further 15-25 minutes (the timing depends on the thickness of the slices, and on your oven). By this time, the "chips" should be browned, crunchy on the outside and puffed. Serve at once.

N O T E

If you are using more than one baking sheet, you will need to switch their positions during baking, so that all the potato pieces bake evenly.

Spicy Oven-Fried Potatoes

· · · · · · · · · · · · · · **V** · · · · · · · · · · · · ·

Serves 2–4

For this spicy variation on oven chips, I like to use all-purpose potatoes. The piquant, crunchy little morsels are good hot or at room temperature, although it's hard to keep them around long enough to cool down. As a nibble with drinks, they are dandy.

1/2 teaspoon ground turmeric
1/2 teaspoon garam masala
1/4 teaspoon ground cumin
a few drops of lemon juice
1 heaped tablespoon tomato
   purée

1 lb potatoes, peeled and cut into
   1/2-inch cubes
olive oil and water spray
   (see page 5)

1 Preheat the oven to 425°F.

2 Whisk together the spices, lemon juice and tomato purée in a large bowl. With two spoons, toss the potato cubes with the spice and tomato mixture until very well coated.

3 Mist a non-stick baking sheet with the oil and water spray. Spread the potatoes out on the tray in one layer, and bake in the oven for 25-35 minutes, turning them once or twice. When they are browned, puffy and tender, they are ready.

Steam-Roasted Potatoes in Parchment Packets

· · · · · · · · · · · · **Ⓥ** · · · · · · · · · · · ·

Serves 1

If you wrap potato cubes in baking parchment and bake the parcels in a hot oven, the potatoes steam as they roast. The potato pieces that rest cut-side down on the parchment turn dark brown and smoky, those that rest skin-side up puff up with steam; the contrast is part of what makes these potatoes so spectacular. Serve as they are, or serve with Colombian Tomato-Cheese Sauce (see page 98), or any sauce you like.

4-5 new potatoes or
   2-3 medium potatoes

olive oil and water spray
   (see page 5)

1 Preheat the oven to 425°F.

2 Scrub the potatoes and dry them. If you are using new potatoes, halve or quarter them. If you are using medium size potatoes, cut them into quarters or eighths. (You need potato pieces of about 1 inch.)

3 Tear off a piece of baking parchment large enough to enfold the potatoes generously. Fold the paper in half and crease it along the fold. Open and mist the paper lightly and evenly with the oil spray. Spread the potato pieces evenly on one half of the paper, some of them cut-side down, some skin-side down. Fold the other half of the paper over and seal securely by folding over and crimping the edges all round and forming a roughly semi-circular parcel (see page 127). The parcel should be roomy but well sealed. Slide the parcel onto a baking sheet, take it to the oven, then slide the parcel off the sheet, directly on to the oven rack. Bake for 30-35 minutes or until the packets are puffy and the smoky aroma of roasting potatoes is driving everyone wild. Slide the parcel onto a platter and open by cutting a cross in the top. Serve at once.

Potato-Wild Mushroom Gratin

· · · · · · · · · · · · · **Ⓥ** · · · · · · · · · · · ·

Serves 2-4

Only 1/2 oz dried porcini *mushrooms is needed to imbue this entire gratin with their wild, woodsy flavor. The top layer of potatoes becomes as crisp as potato crisps, while the under layers are meltingly tender.*

1/2 oz dried *porcini* mushrooms
1 cup warm water
2 large potatoes,
   scrubbed and sliced paper-thin

salt and freshly ground pepper
about 1 teaspoon vegetable
   bouillon powder

1 Preheat the oven to 400°F.

2 Rinse the mushrooms under cold running water, and then let them to soak in warm water for 20 minutes. Tip the mushrooms into a sieve lined with a double layer of muslin or coffee filter papers set over a bowl. Reserve the mushrooms and soaking liquid. Rinse the soaked mushrooms under cold running water, chop them with kitchen scissors and set aside.

3 Arrange a layer of overlapping potato slices on the bottom of a shallow baking dish that will hold the potatoes in three layers. Season with a little salt and pepper, and sprinkle evenly with half the mushrooms. Cover with another layer of potatoes, season, and sprinkle with the remaining mushrooms. Top with the remainder of the potatoes and season lightly with salt and pepper.

4 Stir the bouillon powder into the reserved mushroom liquid in a saucepan, and bring to a boil. Pour over the potatoes. Cover with foil (shiny side in) and bake in the oven for 15 minutes.

5 Uncover and bake for a further 30-40 minutes or until the liquid is absorbed, the under layers are meltingly tender (check with the tip of a small, sharp knife) and the top is crisp. Serve at once.

Potato Frittata

. . . .

Serves 2

Frittata is the Italian name for an open-faced omelette that can be filled with almost any savory mixture. I have eliminated half of the egg yolks (see box), but if you have been told to curtail your dietary cholesterol drastically, it would be best to give this recipe a miss.

I large potato, scrubbed and diced	2 egg whites
I large onion, chopped	2-3 tablespoons chopped fresh
I garlic clove, crushed	parsley
I cup vegetable stock	salt and freshly ground pepper
oil and water spray (see page 5)	2 tablespoons grated Parmesan,
2 eggs	low-fat cheddar
	or Swiss cheese

1 Put the potato, onion, garlic and stock in an 8- to 10-inch non-stick frying pan. Cover and boil for 5 minutes.

2 Uncover, reduce the heat and simmer until the stock is almost gone and the vegetables are tender. Scrape the mixture into a bowl, wipe out the pan, then mist with the oil spray.

3 Preheat the grill. Beat the eggs and the egg whites together with the parsley, and season with salt and pepper. Heat the pan and pour in the egg mixture. Cook over medium heat, without stirring, for a few seconds or until the eggs begin to set on the bottom, then spoon in the potato mixture.

4 With a flexible plastic spatula, lift the edges of the omelette away from the pan, and tilt the pan so that the uncooked egg flows beneath the cooked portion. Continue doing this all around the pan until the omelette is almost completely set.

5 Sprinkle the top of the omelette with cheese. Broil for 2-3 minutes to set, melt the cheese, and very lightly brown the top. Serve at once, in wedges, straight from the pan.

WHAT TO DO WITH LEFTOVER EGG YOLKS

1 Feed them to your dog. Dogs metabolize fat and cholesterol differently from humans. The yolks will make your dog's coat shine.

2 Find a book on natural beauty remedies and learn how to make egg yolk hair and skin lotions.

3 Make egg tempera from the yolks, and paint beautiful pictures (see an artist's manual for directions).

Potato-Fennel Gratin

· · · · · · · · · · · · **V** · · · · · · · · · · · ·

Serves 2–4

Substitute fennel for the porcini *used in the recipe on page 177, and the potatoes take on a gentle anise character.*

2 potatoes, scrubbed
  and sliced paper-thin
2 fennel bulbs, trimmed and cut
  across into paper-thin slices

about 1 cup boiling vegetable stock
freshly ground pepper

1 Preheat the oven to 400°F.

2 Arrange overlapping rows of potato slices and fennel slices in a single layer in a gratin dish. Pour 1 cup hot stock evenly over the vegetables, season with pepper and cover with foil, shiny side in.

3 Bake in the oven for 15 minutes. Uncover and bake for a further 15-25 minutes or until the vegetables are tender, brushing the potatoes with stock (use a pastry brush) occasionally during the last 5-10 minutes.

Potato Chili

. . . .

Makes 4 cups

Chili doesn't have to be con carne! *It can be* con patate, *as well. This dish can be made ahead of time and reheated at serving time; the flavor will only improve, although you may have to thin it with a bit of stock before reheating.*

2 cups vegetable stock
3 large onions, halved and sliced
　into thin halfmoons
2 garlic cloves, crushed
I teaspoon each of dried oregano
　(crumbled), ground cilantro,
　mild chili powder and
　ground cumin
I tablespoon paprika
cayenne, to taste
3 heaped tablespoons tomato
　purée
3 large potatoes, scrubbed, halved
　and cut into I 1/2-inch chunks
salt and freshly ground pepper

grated Parmesan or
　low-fat cheddar cheese and
　cottage cheese, to serve

PEPPER SALAD
3 large peppers (I red, I yellow,
　I green), peeled, deseeded
　and diced
3 thin scallions, sliced
I tablespoon chopped fresh
　parsley
1/2 tablespoon chopped fresh
　cilantro
juice of I lime
salt
1/2 teaspoon sugar

1 Put 1 cup of the stock in a flameproof casserole with the onions, garlic, herbs and spices. Cover and boil for 10 minutes.

2 Uncover and cook for 5-7 minutes or until the onions are tender and the liquid has almost cooked away. Blend in the tomato purée.

3 Stir the potatoes into the onion mixture, season with salt and pepper, then pour in the remaining stock. Bring to a simmer, stirring. Partially cover and simmer for 45-55 minutes or until the potatoes are tender and the sauce is very thick and rich.

4 Meanwhile, to make the pepper salad, toss all the ingredients together in a bowl at least 30 minutes before serving.

5 Serve the chili in shallow soup bowls. Top each serving with a sprinkling of cheese, a dollop of cottage cheese, and a spoonful of pepper salad.

V Serve without the cheese or cottage cheese garnish.

Colorful Potato Vegetable Casserole

Makes 7 cups

It's not necessary to peel the potatoes, but the peppers—as always—are much improved if peeled. This casserole is exceptionally aromatic.

5 medium potatoes,
    scrubbed and thickly sliced
2 medium onions, halved and sliced
    into thick halfmoons
2 large yellow peppers, peeled
    and cut into 1-inch chunks
3 celery stalks, cut into
    2-inch pieces
1 fennel bulb, cut into eighths

2 14-oz cans of Italian peeled
    tomatoes, well drained and
    crushed with the fingers
1 fresh chile, deseeded and chopped
a handful of basil leaves, shredded
2 tablespoons finely chopped
    fresh parsley
salt and freshly ground pepper
olive oil and water spray
    (see page 5)

1 Preheat the oven to 450°F.

2 Put the potatoes and onions in a bowl, add all the remaining ingredients except the oil spray, and toss to mix. Mist lightly with the oil spray and toss once more. Spread the mixture in a gratin dish and cover tightly with foil.

3 Bake in the oven for 45-50 minutes or until the potatoes, celery and fennel are very tender.

Smoked Tofu and Potato Salad

· · · · · · · · · · · · · **Ⓥ** · · · · · · · · · · · · · ·

Makes 5 cups

Potato salads are usually dressed in one of two ways: with a vinaigrette or with mayonnaise. In place of vinaigrette, try an infusion of stock, sun-dried tomatoes and garlic, combined with balsamic vinegar as in this recipe. In the two recipes following this one, cottage cheese stands in nicely for mayonnaise.

1 1/2 lb new potatoes, scrubbed
1/2 lb smoked tofu, cubed
1 tablespoon capers, drained
1 grilled pepper (see page 131), deseeded and diced (roasted peppers from a jar or can may be used) or 1 fresh red pepper, peeled, deseeded and diced
2 tablespoons balsamic vinegar

1 cup vegetable stock
3-4 dry-packed sun-dried tomatoes, finely diced (use scissors)
1-2 pinches of crushed dried chilies
1 garlic clove, crushed
freshly ground pepper
2 tablespoons chopped fresh parsley
3 scallions, cut in half lengthwise, then thinly sliced across

1 Steam the potatoes over boiling water until tender but not falling apart. Halve or quarter them.

2 While the potatoes are still warm, gently toss them with the smoked tofu, capers and peppers in a bowl. Add the balsamic vinegar and toss well.

3 Put the stock, tomatoes, chile and garlic in a small frying pan. Boil rapidly until the liquid is reduced by half. Immediately pour the stock mixture over the potatoes. With two wooden spoons, gently turn the potatoes so that they are coated with the stock mixture. Season with pepper. Mix in the parsley and scallions just before serving.

Spicy Potato Salad

· · · · · · · · · · · · **Ⓥ** · · · · · · · · · · · ·

Makes 5 cups

The secret of this potato salad and the next is lime juice, teriyaki sauce, and lively seasonings added to the potatoes while they are still warm, so the flavor penetrates right through. Finally, fold in the creamy cottage cheese dressing.

1 1/2 lb potatoes, scrubbed
2 tablespoons fresh lime or
   lemon juice
1 teaspoon teriyaki sauce
1-2 pinches cayenne
   (optional)
1/2 teaspoon ground cumin
2 celery stalks, diced
1 carrot, coarsely grated
1 red pepper, peeled, deseeded
   and diced
salt and freshly ground pepper

DRESSING
5 tablespoons very low-fat cottage
   cheese
3 scallions, thinly sliced
1 tablespoon snipped fresh chives
1 tablespoon chopped fresh parsley

1 Steam the potatoes over boiling water until tender but not mushy.

2 Meanwhile, to make the dressing, combine all the ingredients thoroughly.

3 While still warm, cut the potatoes into 1-inch cubes and transfer to a bowl. Add the lime or lemon juice, teriyaki sauce and spices, and toss well.

4 Add all the remaining ingredients and the dressing and toss gently to combine.

Chickpea and Potato Salad

. . . .

Makes 5 cups

Potatoes and chickpeas make good companions, particularly in a salad. Serve garnished with one of the tomato relishes (see pages 187-89) for beautiful color.

I lb potatoes, scrubbed
I 15-oz can of chickpeas, drained
   and rinsed
2 tablespoons fresh lime juice
I teaspoon teriyaki sauce

1/2 teaspoon ground cumin
3 scallions, thinly sliced
2 tablespoons chopped fresh parsley
4 tablespoons cottage cheese

I Steam the potatoes over boiling water until tender but not mushy. When cool enough to handle, cut into 1/2-inch cubes and transfer to a bowl.

2 Add the chickpeas to the potatoes. Stir together the lime juice, teriyaki sauce and cumin, and pour over the potatoes and chickpeas. Toss gently with two spoons so that they absorb the liquid. Stir in the scallions and parsley. Allow to cool.

3 Finally, gently fold the cottage cheese into the salad.

Relishes, Raitas, Salsas and Chutneys

These are the extra little fillips that provide the final note of texture, flavor and color to a vegetarian meal; the crowning touch to an already bursting-with-personality repast. Most of them are very quick to throw together; make several at once, and keep in the fridge in covered containers to embellish your meals.

Carrot Raisin Chutney

. . . . **Ⓥ** . . . .

Makes 2 cups

You might find yourself eating this simple and refreshing chutney straight out of its container, and why not? It will keep in the fridge for 3-4 days.

6 large carrots, grated
4 tablespoons yellow raisins
4 tablespoons chopped
   fresh parsley

2 tablespoons shredded fresh mint
1/2 teaspoon ground cumin
juice of 2 large lemons and
   2 large oranges

1 Put the grated carrots in a lidded container, and add the raisins parsley and mint.

2 Stir the cumin into the citrus juices, then add the mixture to the carrots. Cover the container and shake well to combine thoroughly. Chill for at least 1 hour before using.

Mexican Salsa

. . . . **Ⓥ** . . . .

Makes 6 cups

A Mexican salsa is used as a salad, relish or sauce. It's great as a zesty garnish to beans and vegetable chilies, and it's good as a dip with pita crisps or tortilla chips, or as a relish in pita pocket sandwiches or wrapped tortillas. It improves with age, so make it ahead of time and let it mellow. The chile and garlic can be increased or eliminated according to your taste. This salsa will keep in the fridge for 4-5 days.

2 28-oz cans of Italian
  tomatoes, well drained
1 14-oz can or jar of red peppers,
  well drained, or 2-3 grilled
  peppers (see page 131),
  or peeled raw peppers
1 fresh chile (or less to taste),
  deseeded and chopped

1/4 cup red wine vinegar
1-2 garlic cloves, crushed
2 tablespoons chopped
  fresh parsley
2 tablespoons chopped fresh mint

Crush the tomatoes with your fingers and put in a bowl. Dice the peppers with kitchen scissors and add to the tomatoes. Add all the remaining ingredients and mix well.

Tomato-Corn Relish

· · · · · · · · · · · · **V** · · · · · · · · · · · · ·

Makes 3 cups

Corn survives processing very well. Frozen corn is excellent, and canned corn is good, too. Use whichever is most convenient. This is another of those compelling salad relishes you will want to eat straight out of the container. It will keep in the fridge for 4-5 days.

8 oz frozen corn kernels,
  cooked briefly and drained
1/2 lb cherry tomatoes, quartered
2 grilled peppers (see page 131),
  deseeded or use canned
  peppers
1 fresh chile deseeded and finely
chopped

salt and freshly ground pepper
1/4 cup balsamic vinegar
1 tablespoon sugar, to taste
2 tablespoons each of chopped
  fresh cilantro, chopped fresh
  parsley and snipped fresh chives

1 Put all the ingredients together in a bowl, and toss until the sugar is dissolved.

2 Spoon into a jar or container, cover and refrigerate until needed.

Cherry Tomato and Cucumber Relish

· · · · · · · · · · · · · Ⓥ · · · · · · · · · · · · ·

Makes 4 cups

The trick to good-tasting cherry tomatoes is to buy them several days before you use them, so that their flavor has time to develop. Don't refrigerate them, or the flavor never arrives. The sweetness and deep tomato character of most cherry tomatoes make them perfect for snacking. I keep a bowl of them out on the kitchen counter at all times, and they disappear very fast. This relish is best eaten on the day it is made, but will keep for a day or so.

18 oz cherry tomatoes, quartered
1 large cucumber, peeled, halved
   lengthwise, deseeded and
   thinly sliced
1 fresh chile, deseeded and
   finely chopped
1 tablespoon small capers,
   drained
2 teaspoons brine from jar
   of capers
1 1/2 teaspoons balsamic vinegar

1-2 garlic cloves, crushed (optional)
juice of 1/2 lime
3 scallions, thinly sliced
2 tablespoons chopped fresh parsley
2 tablespoons chopped fresh
   cilantro
2 tablespoons shredded fresh mint
freshly ground pepper

Put all the ingredients together in a bowl and mix well. Leave to stand at room temperature until serving time, stirring occasionally.

Tomato and Watercress Relish

· · · · · · · · · · · · Ⓥ · · · · · · · · · · · · · ·

Makes 6 halves

Simple, simple, simple, but very effective as to color and taste. Amounts don't really matter, just throw it together—you can't go wrong. This relish does not keep well, so use it on the day it is made.

cherry tomatoes (a mixture of red and yellow, if you can find them)
watercress

snipped fresh chives or thinly sliced scallions
salt

1 Halve the cherry tomatoes and place in a bowl.

2 Steam the watercress over boiling water for 10 seconds. Immediately rinse well under cold running water, and shake dry. Trim off any woody stems, and cut or tear the remaining stems and leaves into 1-inch pieces. Add to the tomatoes.

3 Add the chives or scallions and toss the mixture together. Leave to stand for about 1 hour. Just before serving, salt lightly and toss again.

Fruit and Fennel Chutney

· · · · · · · · · · · · **V** · · · · · · · · · · · ·

Makes 1 1/2 cups

The combination of fragrant, juicy mango with anise-flavored, crisp fennel, spiked with a touch of chili, makes this fruity chutney so memorable. It will keep for 2-3 days.

I orange, peeled and diced
I ripe mango, diced (see box)
I fennel bulb, diced
1/2 small fresh chile deseeded and chopped, or to taste (optional)
I tablespoon chopped fresh mint

I tablespoon chopped fresh parsley
4 tablespoons orange juice
2 tablespoons lime juice
salt and freshly ground pepper

Put all the ingredients together in a bowl and mix well. Refrigerate until needed.

PREPARING MANGOES

To dice a mango, use a sharp knife to cut the mango as if you were slicing it in half, but cutting just to one side of the large, flat central stone. Slice down again on the other side of the stone. You will now have two half mangoes and the flat centre stone to which quite a bit of mango flesh still clings.

With a small, sharp paring knife, score each mango half lengthwise and crossways, cutting through the flesh all the way to, but not through, the skin. Push out the skin as if you were pushing the mango half inside-out. The mango flesh will stand out in cubes. Slice these cubes off the skin.

Peel the skin from the centre slice left on the stone. Either slice the mango flesh off the stone and use the trimmings in the chutney, or close the door, tie a tea-towel around your neck, lean over the kitchen sink, and gnaw the juicy mango flesh off the stone. It's messy, succulent, and utterly delicious—it's the cook's reward.

Mint and Cilantro Raita

· ·

Makes 1 cup

Raitas are cooling mixtures of yogurt, herbs and seasonings, meant to accompany curries. I use very low-fat cottage cheese instead of yogurt, because it is much thicker and creamier than low-fat yogurt. The three raitas that follow work well as garnishes for vegetable stews (see pages 156-69), or as dips or salad dressings. Depending on which herbs you use, the raitas can work with almost anything, not just curries. If the cottage cheese is fresh, raita will keep in the fridge for 4-5 days.

1 cup very low-fat cottage cheese	1 fresh green chile, deseeded
4 scallions, sliced	and chopped (optional)
1/2-inch piece of ginger,	4 tablespoons shredded fresh
peeled and crushed	mint leaves
	6 tablespoons chopped fresh
	coriander

Put all the ingredients together in a bowl and mix well. Cover and refrigerate until required.

Cucumber Raita

· ·

Makes 6 cups

Cucumber Raita is very cooling, and the texture is wonderful. It makes a great dip or spread, as well as a curry accompaniment.

2 large cucumbers	2 tablespoons chopped fresh
salt	parsley
1 garlic clove, crushed	2 tablespoons shredded fresh mint
2 tablespoons white wine vinegar	1/2 teaspoon ground cumin
1 cup very low-fat cottage cheese	1/2 teaspoon ground cilantro
3 scallions, sliced	freshly ground pepper

I Peel the cucumbers and cut them in half lengthwise. With a teaspoon, scoop out the seeds from each half and discard them. Cut the cucumber halves into slices about 1/4-inch thick. Toss with a little salt and leave in a non-reactive colander to drain for 30 minutes.

2 While the cucumbers are draining, put the garlic and wine vinegar in a non-reactive bowl, and leave to marinate.

3 Rinse the cucumbers and dry very well with paper towels. Stir into the garlic and wine vinegar mixture. Fold in the cottage cheese then fold in all remaining ingredients. Taste and adjust the seasonings. Cover and refrigerate until required.

Creamy Herb Sauce

This is a sort of all-purpose raita that will go nicely with a wide variety of dishes, depending on which herbs you choose to use.

very low-fat cottage cheese
shredded, chopped or snipped
    fresh herbs (good combinations
    are mint and cilantro, mint and
    dill, chives and parsley, thyme and
    tarragon, oregano and basil. Or try
    using just one herb at a time.)

Whisk the cottage cheese and add a generous amount of a single fresh herb or a combination of herbs. Cover and store in the fridge until needed.

VEGAN RAITA

Purée silken tofu in a blender with herbs and seasonings (see Cucumber Raita recipe) to make a creamy non-dairy raita.

Wrap-Ups

Filo is a paper-thin, low-fat pastry available in boxes, chilled or frozen, from supermarkets. Traditionally, filo is prepared by arranging the paper-thin sheets in layers, liberally buttering or oiling between the layers. As a result, most filo dishes are not low-fat choices. However, for a lower-fat version, each layer can be brushed with lightly beaten egg (or egg white, if you must drastically curtail your cholesterol) or—for vegans, *lightly* misted with oil and water spray (see page 5). Prepared this way, filo makes an excellent low-fat wrapping for vegetarian "sausage" rolls, or for little samosa-like turnovers.

Tortillas

. . . .

Makes 6 halves

Tortillas are flat Mexican chapatis made of corn or wheat. They can be found on supermarket shelves, side by side with bread. With a stack of tortillas and a can or two of beans, wonderful meal possibilities lie in store. Here's how to do it:

If you are not going to use the tortillas within a few days of purchase, store them in the freezer, in their wrapper. To prepare (they just need warming), wrap the tortillas (a mixture of corn and wheat, if possible) in foil and warm in a steamer over boiling water for about 5 minutes, or in the oven at 350°F for 10 minutes. (Add an extra 5 minutes if preparing from frozen.) Wrap the warm tortillas in a clean tea-towel or napkin and put on a plate or in a basket. Serve with bowls of beans—Spicy Bean Dip (see page 42), Zesty Beans (see page 105), or Black Beans (see page 111)— along with Mexican Salsa (see page 186), Green Pea Dip (see page 37), Creamy Herb Sauce (see page 192), and brown rice. Have in bowls, as well, shredded low-fat mozzarella (or you could add cubed mozzarella to the bowl of hot beans so the cubes form molten lumps—marvellous!), chopped fresh chile, and sliced scallions. Let everyone spoon combinations of the beans and accompaniments into their tortillas, wrap and eat (supply plenty of napkins).

V Substitute cubes of smoked tofu for the mozzarella.

"Sausage" Rolls

· · · · · · · · · · · · **Z** · · · · · · · · · · · · · ·

Makes 12 rolls

Suitable fillings for these include Lentil "Bolognese" Sauce (see page 97) with some breadcrumbs added to bind it. Duxelles (see page 36) is excellent as well (no breadcrumbs needed). The rolls can be prepared up to the end of step 3, and then frozen. To bake from frozen, add 5 minutes to the baking time.

1 14-oz package filo pastry, thawed if frozen	filling of your choice (see above)
1 egg, lightly beaten	oil and water spray (see page 5)

1 Preheat the oven to 400°F.

2 Put a piece of plastic wrap on your work surface. Unwrap and unroll the filo (a package will contain about 12 sheets), put it on the plastic wrap, and cover well with another piece of plastic wrap. (The pastry will dry out quickly if left uncovered, so keep covered at all times.)

3 Remove a single sheet of filo from the stack, and spread it flat on the work surface. Lightly brush it with beaten egg, leaving a 1-inch border all around. Spread 1 tablespoon of the filling in a strip where the egg wash begins along one short side. Roll the pastry around the filling, and continue rolling it up to form a tube shape. Crimp and twist the ends of the tube. Don't wrap too tightly, because the filling will expand a bit while baking. Put seam-side down on a *non-stick* baking sheet that you have misted lightly with oil and water spray. Mist the top of the roll lightly with oil and water spray. Repeat until the filo and filling are used up.

4 Bake in the oven for 10-15 minutes or until golden brown, sizzling and puffed. Check once during baking: shake the tray, and if any rolls seem to be sticking, loosen them with a spatula or palette knife and change their position.

Samosas

· · · · · · · · · · · · **7** · · · · · · · · · · · ·

Makes 12

Any of the vegetable curries or chilies on pages 156-65 make good fillings for these samosas, as does Duxelles (see page 36). The fillings used to stuff Cabbage Parcels (see page 118) and Spinach-Rice Pie (see page 56) are both fine, too. At the end of step 3, the samosas can be wrapped and refrigerated for a day or two, or frozen for months. To bake frozen samosas, add an extra 5 minutes to the baking time.

I package filo pastry, thawed
   if frozen
I egg, lightly beaten

oil and water spray (see page 5)
filling of your choice (see above)

I Preheat the oven to 375°F.

2 Put a piece of plastic wrap on your work surface. Unwrap and unroll the filo (a package will contain about 12 sheets), put it on the plastic wrap, and cover with a second piece of plastic wrap. (The pastry will dry out quickly if left uncovered, so keep covered at all times.)

3 Take one piece of filo from the stack and spread it out on a work surface. Lightly brush the sheet with beaten egg. Fold the bottom third of the pastry up, and then the top third down, as if folding a business letter (see illustration opposite). Brush again with egg. Place a generous tablespoon of filling on the lower right-hand corner, and fold the top right-hand corner down to cover it and to form a triangle. Brush with more beaten egg. Fold the triangle over to form a new triangle, and brush with egg again. Continue folding and brushing lightly until you have formed a many-layered triangle. Mist the finished triangle lightly with oil spray and place on a non-stick baking sheet that you have misted lightly with oil spray. Make more samosas until all the pastry sheets and filling are used up.

4 Bake in the oven for 20-30 minutes or until puffed up and golden. Serve at once.

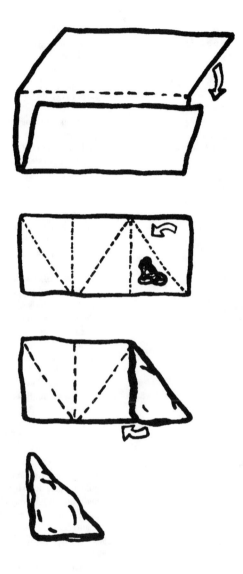

Index

Thank you so much to Sandie Mitchel-King who tackled the manuscript on short notice, enabled me to meet a demanding (you want it when?!) and sailed through the whole thing with her usual competence and aplomb.

Thanks too, to my son Shawn who showed up unexpectedly at my front door just when I needed him the most, and to my husband Steve who keeps me nutritionally correct.

I am grateful to Snakehall Farm (The Prospect Trust) for supplying incomparable vegetables in season and to their garden team for keeping my garden bristling with herbs.

And finally, thank you to David Grossman who managed to pull me out of the doldrums, Vicki Kimm who cares deeply about vegetarianism and is always happy to talk about (vegan) food, and to Brenda Huebler who—as always—helps in many ways.

Identification of Photographs following page 108

Photo A Colorful Corn Chowder (page 25), Chunky Grilled Pepper Gazpacho with Tomato Sorbet (page 31) and Olive-Sun-dried Tomato-Lentil Spread (page 40)

Photo B Stir-Fried Asparagus (page 154), Pan-Fried Wild Rice Fritters (page 52) and Pan-Fried Brown Rice Fritters (page 53) on a plate with Creamy Mushroom Ragout (page 167) and Cherry Tomato and Cucumber Relish (page 188)

Photo C Pasta with Fresh Vegetable Sauce (page 82), Lentil "Bolognese" Sauce (page 97) served with spaghetti

Photo D Tomato and Watercress Relish (page 189), Stir-Fried Peppers (page 151), Savory Polenta Pie with Garlic and Scallions (page 80) on a plate with Eggplant Bean Stew (page 110)

Photo E Cauliflower and Peppers (page 152), Bread and Caramelized Onion Pudding (page 88), Italian Sweet and Sour Zucchini (page 149)

Photo F Sweet Rice Pulao (page 60), Fruit and Fennel Chutney (page 190), Vegetable Curry with Corn Cobs (page 162), Mint and Cilantro Riata (page 191), Green Split Pea Dhal (page 113)

Photo G Grilled Vegetable Mosaic (page 133), Potato-Wild Mushroom Gratin (page 177)

Photo H Oven-Fried Potatoes (page 175), Mexican Salsa (page 186) filled tortillas (page 194), Black Beans (page 111), Green Pea Dip (page 37)